# Soul-to-Soul

# Soul-to-Soul

Married Couples Stories About
Growing Together
and Becoming One with God

CHERYL POLOTE-WILLIAMSON &
RUSSELL WILLIAMSON, SR.

purposely
created
PUBLISHING

**SOUL-TO-SOUL**
Published by Purposely Created Publishing Group™
Copyright © 2019 Cheryl Polote-Williamson
All rights reserved.

Printed in the United States of America

ISBN: 978-1-64484-000-9

Special discounts are available on bulk quantity purchases by book clubs, associations and special interest groups. For details email: sales@publishyourgift.com or call (888) 949-6228.

*For information logon to:*
www.PublishYourGift.com

# Table of Contents

# Foreword

One of the most critical skills we can have on this planet is being able to establish a relationship—a romantic, business, or platonic relationship. This is something we've shared not only as our personal belief, but also as a teaching point in coaching and guiding individuals to meaningful, lasting connections. The ability to create healthy bonds that can lead to blissful partnerships fortified by effective communication, especially in marriage, is quite elusive but not impossible. While the innate skill to attract the right person and successfully share the same space—simultaneously learning, growing, creating, and even working together seems rare, with the proper guidance, it can be developed and maintained in nearly anyone seeking dedicated commitment. When we found out Russell and Cheryl shared this belief and desired to teach other couples through mentorship as well as provide a practical guide for single hopefuls, we were glad to show our support for *Soul-to-Soul*—a book we are sure will inspire and encourage others with stories of triumph. We are excited about successful couples sharing how they have grown, developed, and overcome marital problems, nurtured their relationships, built effective communication channels, applied biblical principles, or labored to become the couple they desired.

We are by no means perfect. You'll discover that the couples sharing their personal journeys and advice in this book do not profess being so either. However, we have all figured out how to communicate in a positive way that pushes our families forward and allows us to thrive. You'll read stories of couples that are in ministry together, work together, or serve together. I know with our family, we manage to do these things and still keep family first. It requires skill and balance, but it is doable. And Russell and Cheryl, along with seven other couples, want to show you how. It's time to have real conversations. It's time to develop the hard skills that will be key in your relationships. Let's get *Soul-to-Soul* and let real couples with real examples show you how!

**Jill and Paul Brunson**
Author
Entrepreneur
NAACP Image Award Winner
Relationship and Life Coach
Television Personality
Matchmaker Expert

# United We Stand, Together We Will Not Fall

## SHIRLEY WALKER-KING AND VINCENT D. KING

*"Therefore what God has joined together, let no one separate."*

—Mark 10:9 (NIV)

As with the military, a lasting marriage requires honor, courage, and commitment. Love is truly a battlefield. At some point in your marriage you will be fighting a war, winning a war, as well as sharing the victory and defeat of "marital warfare." But, even defeat can be turned into a victory when you have God on your side. So, grab your holy water and armor up!

As people, we all come with baggage and imperfections. We will make mistakes, and we will ask and sometimes beg for forgiveness at some point in all relationships, including marriage. Being married to a military person, well that creates a new category for warfare. The military lifestyle brings about many uncertainties for a marriage. Being in a military marriage requires extra tender love and care. You find yourself feeling like you have no say in your own life. You have to learn to roll with the punches, or in the military world, the orders. Orders are the way the military communicates instructions. They tell you what to do, how to do it, and when it will be done. No if, ands, or buts. Dealing with military orders can be very frustrating for the entire family. As the spouse, you may feel you have no say-so in how you live, where you live, and how long you will live there. For the active duty personnel, you may feel guilty asking your family to put your career first; but, the uniform comes first. It takes priority over everything else. It may not always be that way, but while your spouse serves in uniform the family makes many scarifies, willing or unwilling. So, saying communication is the key to a successful military marriage is an understatement.

In order to survive the battlefield of love and marriage while serving in the military, we created the Marital Rules of Engagement. We had to learn how to truly communicate, respect, trust, love, forgive, and stay committed to each other on the battlefield of marriage. Now we would like to share with you our strategies for having and maintaining a healthy marriage and relationship.

- ▸ Marital Rule of Engagement #1 - Communication
- ▸ Marital Rule of Engagement #2 - Respect
- ▸ Marital Rule of Engagement #3 - Trust
- ▸ Marital Rule of Engagement #4 - Love
- ▸ Marital Rule of Engagement #5 - Forgiveness
- ▸ Marital Rule of Engagement #6 - Commitment
- ▸ Marital Rule of Engagement #7 - Faith

Keep in mind that men and women may have a different understanding of what each of these words mean; so, we will begin some rules by giving you the Merriam-Webster's

Dictionary definition, then breaking them down to what we, The King's, translate them to mean.

**Communication** as defined by the Merriam-Webster's Dictionary is a "process by which information is exchanged between individuals through a common system of symbols, signs or behavior." We like to emphasize that in a marriage communication requires listening more than you talk. And please remember that listening is not the same thing as hearing. Hearing refers to the sounds you hear. But, when it comes to listening to your spouse, it requires more than that... it requires focus. Listening means paying attention to not only the words they say but to the message, the meaning, and the delivery. It requires you to pay attention to his or her body language in and out of the bedroom. Having a lasting marriage requires you to listen to learn as you learn to listen. When you communicate with your spouse you must practice active listening: listen to understand, listen without judgment, and don't interrupt.

## 1. Practice active listening

"If we were supposed to talk more than we listen, we would have two tongues and one ear."—Mark Twain

When you are actively listening to your partner, you will be inclined to ask clarifying questions such as: "What I hear you saying is _____." or "Did you mean _____?"

## 2. Listen to understand and show you understood

Listening to understand means that you are not forming your response in your mind. Acknowledge what is being said with a nod, a yes, or an okay. This may seem trivial, but it shows that you are engaged in what is being said and that you comprehend the message.

## 3. Listen without judgment

Listening without judgment is crucial to a marriage. You have to be open and receptive to what is being said. You have to learn to control your body language, your eye contact, and in some cases rolling your eyes, folding your arms, and shaking your leg in disagreement. Those actions can be very distracting and prevent your partner from opening up in the future.

## 4. Don't interrupt

The goal is to give the person speaking the floor. Let them speak uninterrupted without your ifs, ands, buts, or statements like: "If you would have..." or "That didn't stop you from doing..." This is not the time for a debate. This is the time to try to understand the other person's point of view. Try to let go of preconceived ideas and reasoning. It is very important to express negative feelings constructively. If and when your spouse says something you disagree with, wait until it's your turn to talk. Once you have the floor, you should repeat what you heard them say to make sure you are on the same page. Ask clarifying questions like: "Could you clarify what you meant by_____?" Communicate with open-ended questions such as: "When did you first start feeling like this?" If what was said seemed like a bunch of mumbo jumbo, then say that; but, say it without an attitude. Try saying, "I'm not sure I understand what you are saying." Or "I don't feel clear about the main issue here." When the lines of trust have been crossed, it is very important to be honest and upfront with questions like: "What will you do to regain my trust?" and "Do you promise to be honest?" If your situation is greater than the two of you can handle, you should seek outside help from a certified or licensed counselor or therapist. Remember that with God, counseling, and careful and constructive communication any marriage can be renewed, restored, and refreshed.

**Respect** in a marriage is the center of it all! Vincent learned the values of respect from his military career mainly during Basic Training. His father was in the Army, so he knew it was in his blood and he could complete any challenge put before him. However, the fear of failing Basic Training (boot camp) was still there. During the process, that fear gradually became respect. He soon realized military boot camp is not designed to just break you down, but to build you up and create a family of individuals trained to be one fighting force. Completing military boot camp training will push you beyond your fears and doubts and allow you to accomplish more than you ever thought possible. The military teaches you that you must not only have respect for yourself, but you must learn to have respect for others even when you don't have the same beliefs, political affiliations, culture, or background. Without respect there is no cohesiveness, especially as it pertains to marriage.

From the very beginning of our relationship, Shirley has stated that "having respect for each other will go further than love." That statement is not easily understood until you fall out of love with your spouse's personality but still have respect for their character. Couples may fall in and out of love, but ultimately respect must always be present. The lyrics from the great Al Green's song "Love and Happiness" said, "Love will make you do right, love will make you do wrong." However, in most circumstances, respect will eliminate doing wrong. Respect keeps a person focused on family. It makes them think about how their children would view their mistakes, comments, and actions. "In everything set them an example by doing what is good. In your teaching show integrity, seriousness..."—Titus 2:7 (NIV)

It is vitally important that your children see the respect you show to one another so that they will retain that and reciprocate it in their relationships. As a man, it is your responsibility to show a boy how to be a man. And as a woman, it is your responsibility to show a girl how to be a lady. They are watching you. Just think about how much you witnessed as a child that you wish you could have changed. Most of us come from blended families. If you're lucky, you were raised in a two parent, well-rounded household and your parents were able to shelter you from bad adult behavior. But if you are like the rest of us, you have been exposed to conflict, disagreements, and negative talk. We decided early in our relationship to never speak negatively, loudly, or disrespectfully to each other and without a doubt never in front of our child. Yes, we live in the real world too and things do happen. People get upset, attitudes flare up, tempers rise and all that, but we decided to break the chains of dysfunctional communication. In doing so, we created CTO, which stands for Couples Time Out. In this Couples Time Out we have three rules:

**Rule #1**: Once a time out has been called, it's non-negotiable. Both parties must immediately stop the conversation. No ifs, ands, or buts. This is done to keep each party from saying something he or she might regret. Stopping the conversation or disagreement should be used to buy time to build your case. It should be used when one or both of the parties feels the conversation is going nowhere, about to get nasty, or when emotions are too far gone to control. The time out could consist of you going to separate rooms to cool down, gain composure, take a walk, drive, or just scream. Keep in mind that calling a Couples Time Out takes knowing yourself and your partner's triggers. The only rule is to let the other party know why you feel a time out is needed and for how long.

**Rule #2**: Generally, the Couples Time-Out should not be taken for longer than two days... generally. During this time, each person should put themselves in the other person's shoes. Try to reflect on how the struggling person might feel. You may not have any sympathy for your partner's poor judgment, misunderstanding, or wrongdoing, but try to be empathetic. Again, calling the Couples Time Out is meant to allow tempers to cool down not to bury the issues. Any attempts to bury the issues should be brought up with good intentions while keeping each other's stress level and health in mind. Couples Time Out doesn't mean you are free and clear from the conflict, it is just a pause for the cause to keep some level of peace while you work at resolving your issues.

**Rule #3**: Once the time out is over, both parties must come back to the conversation ready to discuss the topic at hand. Ready to deal with the issues. Each party should come back with open ears, an open heart, and a safe tone. Each party should have an opportunity to restate or summarize their understanding of what the other person said, felt, or did. Be prepared to use active listening. Offer apologies and accept wrongdoing and or solutions. Remember Couples Time Outs are a temporary fix designed to help, heal, and resolve conflicts.

The bottom line is that you must respect your partner the way you want them to respect you.

**Trust** in a relationship is earned. Trust is something that is built over time and is a very important component of a healthy marriage. Trust comes with being honest, responsible, and reliable. When you trust your partner, you feel safe and secure both emotionally and physically. You have their back, and they have yours. The goal is to be loyal to your partner through thick and thin. You want your partner to be your "ride or die." In order to create that kind of trust, you must do these four things:

**Don't keep secrets**: You have to be open and honest from the beginning. Respect each other's differences and keep people out of your business. Keep your private conversations private. Tell the truth.

**Do what you say and say what you are going to do**: The best way to say this is to make sure your actions match your words. Don't just say you love me, show me. Be sincere about your actions and reactions. Live with integrity and integrity will live with you!

**Stay faithful**: Make your relationship the top priority. Don't just say you're loyal, show your loyalty by being faithfully committed in all aspects of marriage. Be clear about boundaries and expectations.

**Be forgiving**: Everyone deserves a chance to make things right. Learn to accept an apology. Trusting someone doesn't mean you forgot about the situations, mistakes, or triggers. It simply means you forgave them so that you don't have to carry their guilt.

When you fall in love with the character of the person you are married to, you can trust that he or she has your best interest at heart and will protect and guard your trust as his or her own. That's how you stay married for life—trust!

**Love** is a daily commitment. In a marriage, love is like a sixth sense. When it comes to love in a marriage you can't get lazy. Laziness in a marriage leads to disconnection and disaster. When you become one, staying in love requires work. It requires daily affirmations, daily touch, and daily romance! Love as it pertains to marriage is not just a four-letter word. In marriage, you must know you're loved and love yourself to make it last forever.

We were 10 years into our marriage before we clearly identified each other's love languages. While taking a class, Shirley was introduced to Gary Chapman's book *The Five Love Languages*. She came rushing into the house after her night class with extreme energy and excitement and said, "I get it, I finally get it; your love language is touch!" As I stood there looking at her as she had what seemed to me to be a bizarre moment, she continued by shoving this book into my face while pointing at the pages and reading it passionately and flamboyantly. She was determined to break it down to me right then and there. Needless to say, for the next two weeks we read and studied this book together. We had our aha moments page by page. Discovering our love languages gave us renewed purpose. From that day forward, we agreed to wholeheartedly communicate to each other using each other's love language.

My primary love language is physical touch, with quality time coming in a strong second. Which means, I'm a hands-on, touchy-feely type of guy. Shirley now communicates with me by taking time for just the two of us, holding hands, snuggling, and just being one soul. Shirley always remembers the little things, which explains her primary love language of acts of service. It is very important for me to show her my love and appreciation with my actions because the phrase "Actions speak louder than words" fully describes Shirley! So, I show her my love and appreciation with my daily actions, thoughts, and gestures. Knowing your love language is important but knowing the love language of your spouse is imperative for longevity and asking for forgiveness.

**Forgiveness** as defined in the Merriam-Webster's Dictionary is "to stop feeling anger toward (someone who has done something wrong); to stop blaming (someone); to stop feeling anger about (something); to **forgive** someone for (something wrong)." All of that is easier said than done. In order to truly forgive, sometimes it requires taking your pride, feelings, and insecurities out of the equation. Asking for and granting forgiveness in a marriage can take the love, fear, and divine intervention of God. In a marriage, asking for forgiveness and saying I'm sorry is inevitable. Unfortunately, it's just a matter of when, how, and for what.

Being married while in the military creates distance, distance creates distractions, and distractions create lack of trust. Our first distraction was being married in our early twenties while most of our friends were still living the single life. Vincent had a brief time when hanging out seemed more important than being a husband and father. As Vincent said earlier, for me actions speak louder than words. So, to get my point across, Vincent came home to my bags being packed with baby in hand, flight booked, and living arrangements made. He quickly learned that I have a zero tolerance for disrespect and that I will wholeheartedly hold him accountable for his actions. We had a come to Jesus moment, and I forgave him for his indiscretions. I soon learned that in order to keep my husband home without him feeling like he was missing out on hanging with the fellas, our place had to become the hangout house. And being that I played and enjoyed basketball as much or more than Vincent, I had a connection with his friends as well. Our weekend routine became normal— we played pick up or team basketball on Saturdays. We were almost never on the same team, which worked out for us anyway. So, while I played, Vincent watched Valencia. And when he played, I was on the sideline with Valencia or at the park to give her some fresh air.

As we grew in our marriage and the years flew by, we have dealt with other attacks that required forgiveness. We learned to deal with them head on and address the problems that led to the issue and or issues. Over the years we have dealt with family, friends, and enemies attacking our love, marriage, and trust in God's alignment. But, because we stay aligned with God, we pray together, we ask for forgiveness and we forgive, we have lasted 27 years.

**Commitment** in our marriage is non-negotiable. Did you know that statistics show that approximately one in every two marriages in the United States ends in divorce? It's easy to get married; staying married is the lifelong goal. The odds are against marriage from the start. We can all agree, it's easy to be committed when things are going well. I've never met a divorced couple that said, "We were happy and committed." If those two things lined up, they would still be married, right? Staying committed to your marriage requires a strategy. Which is why we want to share our marital survival skills for success.

> **Survival Skill #1**: Communicate Daily – Tell and show each other how much you love and appreciate each other. Talk.
>
> **Survival Skill #2**: Dream – Talk about your dreams and expectations. Let your partner know your wants, needs, and desires!
>
> **Survival Skill #3**: Become Best Friends – Friendship is a very important ingredient in marriage. Keep your sense of humor and support each other.
>
> **Survival Skill #4**: Fight Fair – Learn how to resolve conflict without hitting below the belt. Stick to the issue at hand. Attack and address the problem not your spouse. Respond don't react.

Learning how to respond to a situation is the first step in being committed to your marriage. In our twenty-third year of marriage, our marriage was attacked from both inside and outside of our circle. Lines have been crossed, drawn, and torn to pieces; but, we never gave up or gave in and allowed society to determine our outcome. We are committed to each other until death do us part. No matter how bad it gets, the good has always outweighed the challenges. Trust me, misunderstandings, conflict, and anger are going to occur. Being committed to your marriage without the fear of abandonment or the threat of divorce will allow for almost any situation to be restored.

**Faith** and having a spiritual connection helps to keep the flesh from becoming weak and falling into temptations. No one is sin proof, but having someone or some form of spiritual resources and support can keep a marriage alive. Couples can build their faith by reading, praying, and studying the Word of God together. God desires unity in a marriage, and if you put your faith in Him you will be victorious. Keeping your faith in your marriage means learning how to trust that God will work things out for the good. Know and believe that He has your marriage protected, even in the bad times, because He knows what He is doing. At various times in our marriage, we have had to strongly depend on our faith while praying together and apart. Most people look at us and think we have an effortless marriage, we don't. We make it look effortless because we have put in the time and effort to deal with and tackle the hard times, pain, and difficulties of life. Trust us, it ain't easy. We have squared up against bad people and dumb decisions. But, the one thing we don't do is go to battle without the Holy Spirit on our side. Looking back on some of those battles, we realize God had a plan and prepared us. We just couldn't see through the smoke and dysfunction until we put on our armor and realized that He was in control and this was just a test of faith.

Always remember that marital warfare is inevitable, but you are not alone. Even defeat can be turned into a victory when you have God on your side. So armor up, stand united, and fight the fight.

# The Soul of My Soul
# from God's Soul

## RAQUEL AND TURHAN JONES

*"Be completely humble and gentle; be patient,*
*bearing with one another in love."*

—Ephesians 4:2 (NIV)

## Raquel Jones

When I met him, I didn't know that it would go this far. When I called him my angel, I didn't know why; but, I knew that he would play an intricate part in my journey. When I first met him, all I could remember was his bright smile and joking demeanor. He appeared to be an outgoing person as he approached me while I was standing on the hill, directing traffic. This was one of the times I wanted to run away fast. But, before I could turn away, I saw him coming. I couldn't leave where I was working anyway. I was working an off-duty job at the club, Park Avenue, where I worked every weekend. I saw him in the parking lot a few times before, and I told my friend Stephanie, "I saw this guy, and he is cute." With the strangest look on her face, she replied, "Who? Because you never say that anyone is cute, I've got to see who it is." I told her that he was with the guys in the Mountain Dew truck who were always handing out Mountain Dew sodas in the parking lot. I didn't know the name of the truck. She said, "I am going to tell him!" I said, "Please don't do that. I was just telling you," as I smiled and shook my head to motion no. She did it anyway, of course, and I am grateful that she did. I can still see her now, pointing me out as she flagged him down. I knew what was about to happen. He was going to come over, and I was too shy for that. Plus, it had been a rough night for me on my regular shift in patrol. I had been involved in a scuffle where my uniform was torn, I was sweating, and my uniform was soiled. When he approached me, the encounter wasn't bad at all. I met the beautiful soul loved by all, Turhan. We exchanged numbers. He spelled his name wrong.

We talked on the phone often, but I didn't see him until a month or so after our first encounter. As our relationship grew, it developed into a friendship more than anything else. We were naïve, young, and oblivious about life and true love. Our love was as untamed as we were. Nothing about our relationship was ever orthodox. He already had two sons and I had no children, but I quickly fell in love with his children. We had a son, and he would be our third son. After five years of being together, we got married because we love being together all the time, we are powerful together, and of course we love each other. However, with immaturity, love can get damaged. With pride, love can get abandoned. Without healing your childhood wounds, you can destroy everything great that comes to you.

After we were married, it seemed that we fought about the smallest things. I felt like he needed to mature, but I wasn't looking at me. I was always pointing the finger at him but not pointing it at myself or looking at the part I played. I wasn't changing anything about myself. Instead, I just looked at him like he wasn't right in his way of doing things. There were many things that I needed to ask God to fix inside of me. We weren't praying together even though we were going to church together. We allowed outside interferences into our marriage by telling our troubles to people who didn't want to see us happy.

I spoke about him unkindly and I spoke to him unkindly at times as if his presence got on my nerves, when in actuality all I wanted was for him to be totally present. I am the type of person who is moved by my feelings. So, if I sense something in you that feels unpleasant to me, I have to get away from it. I didn't know that about myself then. But, I didn't know much about myself at all back then, even though I thought I did. I used to think that he didn't care about me or the relationship like he should. I told myself that so it would prove true in my mind. In turn, I subconsciously began to look for the proof that he didn't care about or respect me. But, I could never find it to be true. I began to wonder why I was trying to prove this terrible thing so much. I would not have been invested in a man that didn't care about me. I had been deceived before by a man that would be a mother's worst nightmare for her daughter, and I hadn't healed from it. I was still angry that that guy had gotten over on me. I was angry that I went against my intuition and allowed the bad energy into my life when God told me that the guy was deceitful. I carried a valise of anger, mistrust, and resentment instead of focusing on healing inside. I was unforgiving, so I held on to any minor offense. At times, I did not wait for God to handle it.

Then, that year after we were married in 2004, I was diagnosed with Lupus Nephritis disease (a type of lupus that attacks the kidneys) and nothing was ever the same. I believed that now that I was dealing with this disease, I could prove to him and to myself that he was unconcerned about me. But, again, I would be proven wrong. We both were stricken with sadness and grief. He didn't know how to handle my diagnosis and neither did I. At times, it seemed like we were extremely close. At other times, we seemed far away from each other. We were vibrating on different frequencies, and we both needed healing. We continued with a toxic lifestyle of eating, drinking, and arguing. At times I felt like he needed to bend his pride because of my condition, but instead I bottled up in anger and shut him out. The thing about arguments is that they're always about the same thing, but never about the thing that is underneath the surface. Our arguments were unhealthy for my condition.

The time came when the disease was no longer quiet, and we both could hear it getting louder. It was like a loud speaker, and we were both forced to hear it. We had to do something about our relationship. I began to understand that I needed to change and fix myself or we weren't going to make it because my internal misery would destroy everything. I began to go to God in prayer frequently, asking Him to clean me up. I asked God to clean my heart and open me to forgiveness. What I didn't understand was that forgiveness started with me. As I prayed for God to lead me in the right direction, He led me to meditation. It was in meditation that I could hear God speaking to me. God was telling me to forgive, so that I could be free.

## Turhan Jones

When I met Raquel, I was in the midst of dating; but, I wasn't serious about anyone. I felt like I was getting up in age and I wanted to change; however, I was coming out of a relationship and I needed some time. That feeling of needing a break quickly evaporated once I was realized what was available on the market.

I was working at K104 and working for Mountain Dew. My job was to hand out some of their new products that weren't on the market yet to get a feel for the response. On this particular night, my co-workers and I decided to go to Dallas and hit up a club called Park Avenue. I was pretty familiar with Park Avenue from working at K104, so this was routine for me. As we pulled into the parking lot, there was plenty of traffic and cars were everywhere. I spotted two female police officers. One of them was tall and brown-skinned and the other one was shorter and light-skinned, resembling Bruce Lee. While I was minding my own business and pulling the truck into the club parking lot, the shorter, light-skinned officer flagged me down to get my attention.

She pointed up the hill to the brown-skinned police officer who looked as though she wanted to run away and disappear like the motto of Southwest Airlines: "Wanna get away?" As I approached her, she had apprehensive body language, sweaty palms, and she looked flustered. We shook hands as I introduced myself and she introduced herself. We continued to talk, and I gave her the wrong spelling of my name, Turon, and my pager number. The reason that I gave her the wrong spelling of my name because she was a police officer and I didn't want her running my name. I am sure she did anyway, but I never asked her. It's safe to say that me giving her my pager number proves that this was a long time ago. She gave me her number, so the next day I gave her a call. We proceeded to have a great conversation in which we learned a few things about each other. After a couple of phone calls within a few days, she called me her angel at the end of one of our conversations. After that, I knew this would be something special; but, I was running from it because I didn't know if I was ready to be everything she would want from me. I didn't know if I could live up to the expectations of a relationship, especially with this particular girl.

I wasn't thinking about marriage, it was the furthest thing from my mind. I was just coming out of a relationship that hadn't required me to be a man and make manly decisions. Then, I met Raquel and it was different. She was mature and it was a new feeling. It was time for me to be a responsible, grown man. Being around this woman made me want to be better. Since she was a police officer, I looked at her as a police officer even when she was off work. I learned that I had stereotypes and many misconceptions about police officers.

Raquel didn't come with the games that my previous relationships came with. Her career, her mental state, and her attitude brought a different feeling to my life. She wanted better for me and I didn't know how to receive that. She didn't have a hidden agenda or motives, she just wanted to be with me. She didn't demand anything from me, she was about business, she didn't play games, and she knew what she wanted. I hadn't really been held accountable in a romantic relationship before, and I was accustomed to doing what I wanted, so being with Raquel was not an easy transition for me.

We started out as friends, and I didn't know that it would transition into a beautiful relationship. She meant business, and she made me want to be about my business. She saw potential in me that I didn't see in myself. She didn't degrade me, she helped me. She didn't question me about other women, she was just being my friend. She didn't pressure me to be anything other than what I was, and she didn't try to change me. I had never met a woman like her.

Once our relationship moved to a serious level, we moved in together then we got married. But, we were both underprepared for a life of responsibility—spiritually, emotionally, and financially. We had a party schedule. Every weekend, we looked forward to our date nights, going out for nice dinners, attending parties, and drinking alcohol. We were having a good time. However, drinking alcohol wasn't in line with what God had for us, and it posed a problem for us because we were more likely to engage in arguments if we were intoxicated. Alcohol brought out misunderstandings, hidden feelings, and jealousy.

We talked, she listened, I listened. She is an attentive listener. We could talk for hours, even at four in the morning. That's when we would have the deepest conversations. She and I continued our impetuous drinking, eating, and living. We attended church, but we didn't pray together like we should have. We began to speak to each other carelessly. I had people around me who weren't married, and I had no one to look to for positive reinforcement. If I found myself in a situation, I didn't have any peers to confide in. I didn't want to put our business out on the streets or cast my problems upon other people. I didn't have anyone who could give me mature and trustworthy advice.

I should have been going to my wife instead of going to anyone else. I made idiotic decisions in my choice of words and actions. We began to talk at each other instead of to each other. Our arguments became petty, repetitive, and were mostly about things both of us had said in the past. That kind of behavior keeps a negative cycle going. Nothing starts arguments more than old arguments. My wife began to mature before I did and she told me, "If I am not using foul language with you or talking to you with a lack of respect, you shouldn't be doing it either if we are planning to make this work."

That resonated with me because, for the first time, I saw myself in her shoes and I pictured her speaking to me as I was speaking to her. We didn't know that she was about to be diagnosed with the potentially fatal disease, lupus. When she was diagnosed, the lupus had already affected her kidneys. We were lost, and we didn't know what to do. We were afraid and I didn't have the level of maturity I needed to have to help her deal with the illness.

As she became sicker, having flare-ups and being hospitalized, I was faced with real life. I had to take care of my boys while she was in the hospital, sometimes for months. Sometimes I felt like I was on my own. It seemed like we lived separate lives because she couldn't do many things. Even when she was home, she was continuously sick. I began to think that was going to be our life, and she would never get better. I didn't know how to fix her and she didn't know how to fix herself. Only God would be able to fix her. "Look to the LORD and his strength; seek his face always."—1 Chronicles 16:11 (NIV)

During Raquel's illness, she went through an awakening. And in her search for life, while in a fight for her life, she found her spiritual center. What happened to her was the worst and best thing that happened to our family. The changes within her were contagious and brought about a spiritual change within me too. She had to change her eating habits, so she eliminated meat and dairy from our household, and she stopped drinking alcohol. She started researching natural ways to get better. She learned about meditation and that calmed her spirit, changed her perception, and opened her mind. She began to talk to me all the time about how we had to change what we thought and spoke. She made a change that would change our lifestyle for the better. She recommended that we start praying together. She told me to forgive when I didn't want to and she made me see reasoning.

We both started going straight to God about our worries instead of going to outsiders. We went within ourselves to where God is to know what we needed to do in any given situation. Raquel's illness took us on a long road of pain and suffering. That painful experience was something that was life-changing for us. It was for the better. It made us stronger, it brought us closer together, and more than anything, it brought us to God.

Now our relationship is different. We are focused on building, being healthy, and getting stronger in God. We see now that all of the arguments and being angry at each other is a waste of our time here together. We know that being out of alignment with God puts us out of alignment in our marriage. We communicate like adults instead of arguing and we are honest about how we feel about each other. Most of all, we let go of things that don't serve our higher good and our highest purpose in God.

We value each other's love now, we don't stay angry with each other, and we kiss each other goodbye each time we leave each other's presence. We say "I love you" to each other every day. We take life seriously, and we take how we live our lives sincerely. We live life by my mother's advice not to go to bed mad at each other because no one is promised to wake up. "Teach us to number our days carefully so that we may develop wisdom in our hearts."—Psalm 90:12 (CSB). There was a time when we didn't heed that advice, so we went to bed not speaking to each other after arguments and disagreements, and not saying I love you to one another. We were wasting time when we could have spent it loving on each other instead. We still have disagreements, but we talk about them with respect for each other's feelings and opinions.

We have become more understanding of each other and we support each other. In our journey, we move as one. We trust each other and we don't seek to find wrong in one another. We believe that if one is looking to find wrong and deceit in someone else that is deceitful in itself. We trust God for everything. We have been in situations where we had no money, no car, and no home to live in. In troubled times, we have had to live with both of our mothers, and we are grateful that we had those safe places to live. There were times when Raquel's health was grim, and we didn't know how we would make it through. We prayed to God, manifested life as we sent out powerful thoughts and words, and put our attention on Raquel's healing.

We stuck together through the times when we felt distant from one another, through repossession, through foreclosure, and through unemployment. We laughed through sadness and depression. We didn't run from our adversities; instead, we faced them and lived through the consequences. We won't say that we didn't make the right choices in life because every choice we made led us to the beautiful point where we are right now. We have been married for 14 years now and we feel like we get to love each other more every day. "Then you will call on me and come and pray to me, and I will listen to you."—Jeremiah 29:12 (NIV).

She is the soul of my soul, as he is the soul of my soul.

# Made for Marriage and Ministry

## KALDEJIA AND ROBERT FAULK

$$\infty$$

*"And if one prevail against him, two shall withstand him; and a threefold cord is not quickly broken."*

—Ecclesiastes 4:12 (KJV)

We met in our local church parking lot. A simple inquiry of who he was led to an embarrassing formal introduction by our mutual friend, Sophie. That brief introduction led to an exchange of phone numbers which turned into daily conversations. We had no idea these daily conversations would give way to us beginning a journey toward marriage or ministry. Love can be birthed in the midst of unsuspecting moments. We dated long distance for six months as I attended college in another city and he was active in the military. In the seventh month, we were married. We recently celebrated our thirtieth anniversary with a vow renewal ceremony hosted by our children.

Before meeting my wife, I was in a relationship that I thought would end in marriage. But, I found out that the young lady and I were on two very different foundations. As I recall, she was church conscience, and I was God conscience. Don't get me wrong, she loved God, but we were unequally yoke. When the relationship ended, I was hurt, angry, and confused. I remember coming home from her house and crying out to God for someone who loved Him as much as I did. If not, I would be single like Paul in the Scriptures. A month or so passed and one night during prayer revival week my life changed forever. A mutual friend, Sophie, introduced me to my wife. I remember struggling to ask her for a number to call. Yet, after that we talked almost every night. She was my friend. Someone I could talk about anything with. Within seven months, we were married. Wow, who would have thought a six-month courtship would be celebrated 30 years later?

Our backgrounds included regular church attendance and a personal relationship with Jesus Christ. He attended a Baptist church with family in the county where he was raised. I, on the other hand, attended chapel which is a place of various worship services held on military installations. Our meeting later gave way to him explaining his role as an armorbearer, as I was unfamiliar with the term and the level of care for the leader it involved.

I was not a member of a church or involved in any capacity, but I attended when home visiting on the weekends from college.

Saved at the age of 17, I was a church goer for about two-months before I backslid into sin again. After rededicating my life to Christ on November 30, 1986, I was given a new opportunity for service; so, I committed to serving God in any capacity I could. My wife's conversion was similar yet dramatic. I remember her coming to the prayer week service and coming up to the altar to give her life to Christ.

When our pastor asked her to repeat the sinner's prayer, he laid hands on her head and immediately she was filled with the Holy Spirit and began speaking with a new language. Several minutes later, she was a new creature in Christ. She was my sister in the Lord.

Here I was a new believer in Christ, learning how to be led by the Spirit and not by the flesh. My conversion to Christianity was unexpected. In my mind, salvation or living for the Lord was reserved for my old age when I was through partying. My husband was instrumental in assisting me with my newfound commitment to Christ. His disciplined prayer life, studying of the Word of God, fasting lifestyle, and honor of our leader made him an exemplary role model for me to follow. I admired his commitment to God, our leader, and serving others. He led a life of serving others with humility, grace, and strength. Something I hadn't previously identified with but was drawn to by his display of love for God.

Since the beginning, our marriage has always been centered on our commitment to God and service to His people. It was unclear to us as newlyweds that Robert's role in our local church and service to our leader would impact our marriage and ministry in the future. Robert's service to our leader involved extended and specific times, as well as specific assignments that were outlined prior to our union. For instance, Saturday mornings were spent preparing the leader's vehicle for Sunday worship service, retrieving laundered clothing, and running other errands if necessary. I found this service to be strange and deemed it as a distraction from our time together. Early on, I resented Robert's fortitude and commitment to the leader, and his service to him and his family. His fortitude and commitment to serve in the local church was the catalyst that laid a foundation for us to serve in future years as a team.

Once married, we vowed to always keep God first in our marriage. As newlyweds, we always allowed our relationship with God to be the focus. In the beginning, I was mostly involved in the service of church. My ministry was to our pastor. Serving him as an armorbearer was a demanding task. Saturday mornings were spent serving his personal needs—washing his car or picking up his laundry. At first, my wife did not understand my commitment and service. But later, her understanding was clear. She began to serve in church along with me. We served as greeters, home group leaders, and assistant pastors. Each church assignment and church leadership promotion allowed us to make more of an impact in the lives of others for the kingdom of God.

While serving alongside my husband for thirty years, twenty plus of them as founding pastors of our current church, I have observed the tenacity and resilience needed to serve people in the midst of serving each other. Your three-strand cord to keep your marriage and ministry intact must be Christ. You must rely on Christ to grace and strengthen you for the labor of love on His behalf to others, that includes your spouse. Recognizing and honoring the strengths your mate brings creates a balance that allows you to know that you are not competing for your spouse's attention or being replaced with the people, places, or things that come along with kingdom work.

As we have served these thirty years together, we have learned the meaning of sacrifice, commitment, and perseverance. Because God was first in our lives, we were able to serve each other and others with the love of Christ.

Identifying specific roles in service while doing kingdom work can eliminate strife, confusion, envy, and jealousy between spouses. At the onset of our marriage and ministry, I was determined to support what I believed was my husband's assignment as a priest, prophet, and pastor of our home. I sensed a call on his life while dating and although I was unclear of what it would look like, I knew I would support him in whatever capacity he served. Defined roles allow you to maximize and strategize the best possible ways to render service to others and provide healthy boundaries in your relationships. Serving in ministry prior to founding our church afforded me an up close and personal vantage point to the power of service.

Once we became married, we almost instinctively began to settle into our specific roles. My wife was very supportive of me, our family, and ministry. She was the intercessor and the prophetic voice I trusted. While she was supporting me, God began to show me that she has a calling on her life. When I first approached her about partnering with me in ministry, she did not feel the need to. After a year, the Lord chastised me saying, "I told you to elevate her in this ministry."

I respected my husband's desire to officially give me a role in our local church. However, I knew I was already fulfilling my assignment in our church by supporting the vision and putting hands and feet to what my husband believed we were called to do. I didn't need to formally solidify what I knew in my heart all the while—I would serve the servant of my home and God's house.

Being able to establish roles and boundaries between your marriage and your ministry assignment presents the opportunity to determine the role models and mentors necessary for success in both. We have been blessed to have role models, mentors, and spiritual parents to pattern our marriage and ministry after. Our assurance lies in the Scripture that admonishes us to follow after those who through faith and patience inherit the promise. We believe that having a support system in place for accountability in marriage and ministry strengthens your marital bond and adds surety to ministry partnership.

We learned early on that having solid spiritual models and mentors was essential to our growth as a couple and as ministry partners. It was because of these parameters that our service became the foundation that would influence and bless others. With God as our source and each other as a resource, we learned that giving was the way we experienced and supported the call of service on our lives.

Individual trials, tribulations, and afflictions can compound when the marital partnership also includes ministry partnership. There are key factors for maintaining a healthy ministry partnership when one or both partners are actively engaged in ministry. These factors include: faith, commitment, respect, support, and honor. Faith, the anchor for maintaining the marriage and ministry, must be stoked like embers burning in a flame. Taking the time to be spiritually fed, individually and collectively, will provide the strength to build a strong foundation both in the marriage and within respective ministry roles. Prayer and fasting can lend tremendously to the renewal of the inner strength required to remain focused on continually building a healthy marriage and presenting a healthy model of ministry partnership.

Our faith was the key to all that we started and established in ministry. Through faith, we stepped out with a vision. Whether it was our marriage or ministry, we stayed in faith, knowing that someone had to be Godly at all times. Faith continues to be the cornerstone of our commitment to each other and God. Through unexpected tests such as the death of Robert's parents and my mother, departure of members, and changes in our circle of friends, our resilience has been rooted in our faith and belief that God will continue to remain committed to us in the process.

Commitment to the vows of marriage, with its challenges, is pivotal to building character in each mate. Commitment to each other in the marriage along with specified roles as it relates to serving in ministry must be established to promote vitality in the marriage as well as in the ministry. The couple must actively engage in activities that will promote the solidarity of the union such as: investment in personal development, role models for marriage, and a marriage and ministry team they can pattern themselves after. There is a need to invest time and receive adequate rest to function optimally as they serve others together. The marriage must be the first priority as it was the first commitment made by each spouse.

Our commitment to each other started in marriage. We decided early on that we would never quit on one another. We had each other. When she needed support, I committed to being her greatest fan and she did the same for me. We always supported each other's dreams and goals. People always saw a united front. She could count on me. Her goals were as important as mine. I respected and valued our marriage and ministry.

Mutual respect is instrumental in valuing the gift that each spouse possesses. Identifying the gifts, abilities, and strengths each spouse brings to the marriage are key components to a healthy marriage. These same components will lend to mutual respect for spouses who serve together in the ministry whether individually or as a team. As a ministry team, we have navigated our marriage and ministry based on the strengths of each other's gifts and the ability to perform the necessary duties required in our local church. Because we established mutual respect for our individual gifts and talents early on in our marriage, it was a seamless transition to support our ministry roles while serving other ministries, as well as during the launch of the church we founded.

Respect was a mutual skill that we freely gave to each other. We realized that God had called us as a team. Our service in ministry would best be served by lifting one another up. We shared this belief and conviction with our family, friends, and church. This philosophy has allowed us to change the mindset of all we come in contact with. When you respect people, their vision, dreams, or goals become easy to connect with and embrace as your own.

Support in the marriage is determined by the individuals' needs. At the onset of our marriage, it was evident that my husband was a visionary. He could take a space, envision the layout, and only require the finishing touches to bring that space to life. He has continued visually painting the vision for our family, which now includes our granddaughters (who we like to call our grand princesses), and our church vision moving beyond the twenty plus years we recently celebrated. I support his vision casting by asking what results he anticipates at the conclusion of the vision being birthed. I'm still amazed at his ability to define what only he can see in a manner that others, including myself, can embrace. He in turn has entrusted me to birth the visions for our family and ministry by supporting my creativity and encouraging me to embrace my gifts and abilities, whilst pushing me to be led by God to empower others to embrace their purpose in life. I believe I'm the mitt to his ball. I hold his vision firmly in place, trusting that we will make a home run for the team.

Honor is the ability to appreciate the place someone holds in your life. I both honor my husband as my spouse and my pastor. Honor always takes into account the other person. We put each other first in submission to God. My wife was not really used to someone putting her first. I would open the door for her, walk on the outside next to the curb, and enter our home first to check it out before letting her go in. It took a while for her to accept my motives as authentic. Ephesians 5:21 states, "Submitting yourselves one to another in the fear of God." We both came from families where honor was overlooked and often never expressed. So much so that divorce was prevalent. Therefore, we decided to honor, never dishonor, each other in both our words and actions. We vowed that divorce was not an option. In the beginning, our families felt that we went overboard. However, now they look to us as an example. We outlasted the critics and the skeptics. Because we choose to honor one another, God has blessed us with this testimony for His glory. We are thankful to God for teaching us how to care for, respect, and honor each other with the grace of the Lord. Relationships can be fulfilling and rewarding when couples submit to honor each other in the fear of God.

"And if one prevail against him, two shall withstand him; and a threefold cord is not quickly broken."—Ecclesiastes 4:12 (KJV)

# Intimacy Is the Key to
# True Fulfillment and Happiness

## TYRIA D. AND KENNEITH E. JONES

*"And if one prevail against him, two shall withstand him; and a threefold cord is not quickly broken."*

—Ecclesiastes 4:12

Our life together didn't start out like a fairy tale or anything like you see in the movies. Frankly, that wasn't the type of relationship I was interested in. I'd been down that road before and so had he. In fact, our relationship started with four words, "Ok, I'm on board." Yes, those were the words that sent us down the aisle. Kenneith (Kenny) and I had both been in previous marriages, so we weren't naïve to the possibility that this one could fail too. The difference between this marriage and our previous marriages was our foundation.

Unlike our previous relationships, we were starting on a solid foundation. That foundation was Jesus! We knew that we wanted Him to be the center of everything we did. He would be the very definition of what our marriage was about. We knew that although our lives revolved around each other, Jesus was the cornerstone. From the wedding ceremony to the way we live our lives, we've made the daily choice to keep

Jesus in everything we do. This marriage would be different because we were going into it with our eyes open. There were no preconceived thoughts or ideas about what it was going to be. We both knew what we were getting into and we knew what it would take for this marriage to be successful.

I remember the day Kenny proposed. It was an ordinary day that turned into one that I'll never forget. I started the day as a single mom and ended it engaged to an amazing man of God. When Kenny presented my ring, it was another reminder of the promise we'd made to each other to keep Jesus in the center. My engagement ring has three stones with the biggest stone being in the middle. This is a daily symbol of our commitment to each other and to Jesus.

## The Friendship

Kenny and I had known each other for about seven years when we ventured into our relationship. We had been the best of friends up to this point. When Kenny expressed interest in us beginning a courtship, I was a little hesitant about moving forward. I didn't want to risk damaging our friendship for something that might not work. I had already been in too many bad relationships and I just wanted to keep things the way they were. Change has always been hard for me.

It took me some months of praying before I came to the decision that he was the man for me. Not only did I love Kenny, but I also liked him as a person. I didn't realize then that liking a person had been the missing piece in my other relationships. It's harder to hurt a friend than it is to hurt someone you "fell in love" with and don't know a whole lot about. Over the years we had been communicating, we'd gotten to know each other intimately. There were things he knew about me that I had never shared with anyone else. He knew my likes and dislikes as well as my past hurts and the hidden things in my heart. It was easy to talk to my friend without any pressure of a relationship.

By the time we came to the idea of taking the friendship into relationship status, we were aware of the hurdles we would have to overcome. We both thought that knowing each other so well would make our transition easier. When you share so much with another person, it's easy to begin to feel like they know you as well as you know yourself. Kenny knew the things I experienced as a child as well as the abuse of my adulthood. He was also mindful of my struggles with physical intimacy because of these things. There was nothing I hadn't shared with him in the previous years. The day I walked down the aisle, I was nervous about so many things, but the wedding night was at the forefront of my mind. Would I be able to satisfy my husband? I was very uncomfortable with sex, and I had made that very clear to Kenny. It had always been something that reminded me of past pain. How could we have the most intimacy in our marriage without the physical connection?

## Pain from the Past

I didn't want to view Kenny in the same light as the other men who had hurt me, but that's exactly what I was doing. Instead of entering our marriage with a clean slate, I brought in all the baggage from past relationships. I realized how unfair I was being to him, and I wanted to do something different. I didn't want to lose him because I couldn't get over the pain others had inflicted on my heart. I also didn't want to continue to punish him for things he hadn't done. All he wanted to do was love me, but I didn't know how to let go of the past and trust him with my future. I could only expect him to be ok with my rejection for so long.

A few years ago, our marriage reached a critical point. We both needed answers on how we could make this work. Neither of us was ready to give up and we knew there had to be something we could do. We decided to read the book, *The Five Love Languages*. Although sex wasn't absent in our marriage, it wasn't the beautiful thing that God had meant for it to be between us. We'd gone years struggling with this issue of physical intimacy causing a rift between us. I was tired of feeling like sex with my husband was something I had to do... a duty. I wanted it to be the experience I'd heard others talk about. I didn't quite know how to communicate what I was feeling to Kenny, and I felt like a failure as a wife. Yes, I cooked, cleaned, and did all the other things a wife is supposed to do. Yet, I failed to meet his needs in this one area.

I knew Kenny tried to understand my struggles, and he'd been patient with me as I tried to work through it all, but it was harder each day. He couldn't continue to go on pretending it didn't affect him as much as it did. I wanted so much to please my husband, but it was hard shutting out the memories and reminders. Once we completed *The Five Love Languages* assessment, we found out that Kenny's top love language is physical touch and mine is quality time. Not only was physical intimacy important in our marriage for us to truly be one, but it was an integral part of who he was and what he needed to have his "love tank" filled and to feel loved. I knew that healing from the past was what I needed if I wanted this marriage to be all that God had shown me. Something had to change!

"The husband should fulfill his wife's sexual needs, and the wife should fulfill her husband's needs. The wife gives authority over her body to her husband, and the husband gives authority over his body to his wife."—1 Corinthians 7:3-4 (NLT). On the day we were married, it ceased to be about me. I was not my own anymore, I belonged to Kenny, and I happily gave myself to him. I could no longer think about how I felt or how things affected me alone. God made us one on that day, so his needs became my needs and vice versa. There were things I had to overcome to be pleasing to him. We knew we needed God's help, and prayer was one of the tools He had given us. We prayed daily for God to heal me. Prayer was the first step in helping us to get to a place of healing and freedom in our marriage.

## Kenny's Thoughts

1 Peter 3:7 says, "Husband**s**, likewise, dwell with *them* with understanding, giving honor to the wife, as to the weaker vessel, and as *being* heirs together of the grace of life, that your prayers may not be hindered." Prior to marrying my queen, I knew that God had given me another opportunity to be a husband. When I realized that He had the wife I was supposed to be in covenant with, I knew I had to do something different. In my previous marriages, I realized that I hadn't been the man I was supposed to be. I never had

a role model in my life to show me what it meant to be a good husband. As I began this new life with the woman God had given me, I reflected on the different teachings I had heard about how to be a better man and husband.

One thing I discovered is that you must always remember that the woman you said "I do" to did not immediately come from God to you. Life has been teaching her lessons from the time she came out of the womb until the time she said those same two words to you. Intimacy for a lot of us was taught by way of television, our teenage friends, or by observing those that were in relationships around us. I realize now that even though some good things could've come from those observations, many were not God-taught; therefore, we were exposed and introduced to bad habits, unrealistic expectations, and negative views of marriage.

As I began this relationship with Tyria, I noticed that being with her was different than any other relationship I had encountered. As she stated, there were things from her past that caused her to put up a wall between us. All my efforts to show my wife that I was different from others were blocked because she felt that I was another person who would hurt her. I wanted Tyria to see that I was trying to express my love and be a good husband. I needed her to see that my actions were pure and not meant to harm her.

It was my responsibility, as her husband, to satisfy her intimately. Even though that was at the forefront of my mind, the reality was that it wasn't happening. I was at a loss as to how we could move past this difficult place to true intimacy in our marriage. It was hard to understand how to help Tyria move into a place of freedom.

## A New Reality

Prior to our marriage, it was my thought that I would give my wife the utmost sexual pleasure, but the reality didn't turn out as I believed it would. We were unable to make an intimate connection. I felt that this was my fault because I didn't realize the extent of her brokenness. Although I was aware of her past struggles, I felt that my love would help her to feel safe and secure with me. If anything, our relationship was far less than what either of us expected. My thoughts of who I was as a man and the truth of her past collided like a ton of bricks.

I was awakened to a new set of expectations from my new bride. Despite the many discussions we had about her past hurts, abuses, and pains, I admit that I didn't truly understand the magnitude of what she had endured. It was on a bigger scale than I felt I was capable of handling. I knew we needed help!

Since God gave her to me, I knew I was the one for her both emotionally and intimately. God had equipped me with everything I needed to help her work through the pain and get to the other side of healing. At that point, we made the decision to seek counseling. During the counseling sessions, some things were said that weren't easy to hear. She had endured many devastating things, but she was strong. I knew this was the first step in her healing and our path to overcoming our intimacy issues.

## She Needs Security

On a side note, one thing that a woman needs is security. She needs to know that she is safe in every area of her life. Prior to us getting married, I had many resources, a roof over my head, and a career that paid well; but, once we were married, I realized none of that helps a woman feel secure. Her past included many people who had let her down and caused her not to trust me. Therefore, I made it my priority to show her that I wouldn't hurt her as others had previously.

I often failed at providing her the security that she needed. As she stated earlier, her primary love language is quality time. Once we took *The Five Love Languages* assessment, I realized that I hadn't done a good job filling her "love tank." I believe that this was one of the reasons she didn't feel protected by me. In her eyes, I was failing at meeting one of her basic needs. Men, if you don't know your wife's love language, I strongly recommend that you find it out as soon as possible. As a man, my primary focus was providing for her needs as well as her wants. I thought that if I did that, all would be happy in the home. Unfortunately, I was wrong again.

I had to change my way of thinking to provide what she needed. It's difficult when your wife doesn't trust you or know if your marriage will be able to withstand the test of time. She needed to know I'd be there no matter what happened in the future. She needed to be secure that I wouldn't leave her "hanging" when things got hard. The most important thing she needed to know was that she could depend on me. That required me to give more than basic needs; she needed my time.

Believe me gentlemen, when you tap into the love language of your wife and begin to fill that tank, you will see a different woman. She will begin to glow again, she will begin to praise you as her husband, and she will brag on you to anyone who is willing to listen. I believe that when we pray and begin to communicate with our spouses, it'll take our relationship to places we never dreamed we could reach together. You will go much farther together than if you were not in it together. The intimacy in your marriage will be rejuvenated and refreshed to the point that you will look forward to the communication.

## Reaching Out for Help

Not only did we fast and pray to see change in our marriage, we also continued to be faithful with counseling. We didn't know how long it would take for us to get over this hurdle, but we knew that we weren't giving up on each other or our marriage. Counseling was intimidating at first because it was hard discussing a topic as sensitive as a lack of sexual intimacy in our marriage. Although it was difficult, we knew we had to dig our heels in and do the work. There were assignments we were given and books we were told to read. We were committed to making the necessary changes.

Whether the struggle within your marriage is sexual intimacy, communication, or something else it's important to remember that you're a team. It's easy to wallow in self-pity and only see your side of the situation. Then, you begin to fight each other instead of coming together to fight the problem. We had to realize that we were not each other's enemy. Matthew 19:6 says, "Since they are no longer two but one, let no one split apart what God has joined together." Once we realized that we were not each other's enemy, we began to see many changes in our relationship.

Counseling helped us get to the root of our issues. Yes, we had issues with intimacy, but there were underlying things going on. One of them was our communication. We had different ways of communicating, so it was like we were talking to each other but neither of us really understood what was being said. There was a communication barrier between us. We had to learn how to effectively communicate with each other.

Counseling also showed us where our marriage needed consistent work. But, it was up to us to continue doing the things we learned if we wanted our marriage to be stronger. Some of the things we did were:

▸ We started our days together in prayer
▸ We set aside time every week just to talk
▸ We started going on regular dates
▸ We took time with each other to dream
▸ We affirmed each other instead of criticizing
▸ We continued our counseling sessions
▸ We found books to read that focused on building a stronger marriage

## Healed and Thriving

We realized that we'd been so busy focusing on the main problem that we weren't doing other things that we needed to do. All of our energy had gone into fixing the intimacy issue, so we forgot to just enjoy each other. The more time we spent together doing that, the more we saw a change in how we viewed our marriage. Although we prayed and believed that God would heal our marriage, we still had to do the work that was required.

The steps we took helped us both heal in every area and start anew. We helped each other to work through problems and came out of it stronger than we were when we started our marriage. "Two *are* better than one; because they have a good reward for their labour. For if they fall, the one will lift up his fellow: but woe to him that *is* alone when he falleth; for *he* hath not another to help him up. Again, if two lie together, then they have heat: but how can one be warm *alone*?"—Ecclesiastes 4:9-11 (KJV)

We reached the other side of healing and now we are whole. Our marriage is everything we knew it could be and we're intimately connected in every way. Sex is no longer a dreaded experience, but the beautiful connection God meant for it to be. We have the tools we need to conquer any obstacle we face now or in the future. Once we overcame the many challenges we encountered, we realized that God had placed us together to fulfill an amazing purpose for His kingdom. We no longer focus on ourselves, but the work that He has chosen us to do.

# Friends, How Many of Us Have Them?

## CHERYL AND RUSSELL WILLIAMSON

*"There is no greater love than to lay down one's life for one's friends."*

—John15: 13(NLT)

It may be hard to imagine willingly laying down your life for anyone as an expression of love. Really consider the possibility that you or another person would, without reservation or hesitation, step in to surrender your life in place of another person's—a friend. The current cultural climate indicates that it's really more about self and self-preservation. You only have to turn on your TV, pick up your mobile device, or walk out your front door and within moments you or someone you know can be caught taking a selfie. It really appears that the environment is trending toward the individual as opposed to the collective.

The growing rise of individualism doesn't seem to bode well for marriage. As we know, a marriage is a union of two people, which under most circumstances is intended to be a lifelong partnership. That's certainly what my wife, Cheryl, and I felt when we decided to get married. We felt with every fiber of our being that God had brought us together and it would be a lifelong engagement. We both made a contract, a covenant, to be husband and wife until death do us part. Now, if you are married and reading this you surely have given the making of this contract great consideration, at least I hope you have. However, if you are single with a desire to marry or marry again, really pause and think about that binding agreement.

Cheryl and I have been in a relationship for 28 years and married for 26 of those years. It's because we became friends first that our marriage has endured for more than a quarter of a century. Being friends was not an expressed intention in the beginning as the two of us were getting to know one another. I mean, I don't recall us ever having a conversation saying, "Let's just be friends" or "We should start as friends and see where it goes." Candidly, it was the guiding hand of the Lord. I share that as a lesson learned from reflecting on who I was and what I was looking for during that period of my life.

At the age of 23, my personal plan was to wait until I reached the ripe old age of 30 before I set out on the journey to find my wife. Previously, I had a high school sweetheart and we discussed getting married at some point in the future after she and I graduated from college. I really thought she was the woman that I would marry one day; however, she had different plans which she surprised me with just before I graduated from college. It's funny as I reflect on that now and realize that in those years you think you have it all figured out; but, you know little to nothing about life. Yet, there is a great joy in the ability to think that everything you desire to happen in life will happen. Just don't burden yourself with the stress of when or how it will happen. Life is a bit smoother if you have the wherewithal to keep this in mind.

So, during this period of my life, I was thinking more about settling into my leadership responsibilities as a relatively young military officer and enjoying the free time I had, when available, to take in my new surroundings in North Carolina. I lived in an apartment with a roommate in Fayetteville, North Carolina. When we were off duty at the same time, we would always look for places to meet new people and make connections with people in our community. If there was a party happening and a good time to be had, we would find it and most definitely participate in the festivities. The last thing on my mind was to find the woman I would wish to spend the rest of my life with; but, God had another plan for me and I'm thankful He is in control.

My roommate and I headed to Raleigh (a 90-minute drive from our house in Fayetteville. We were serious about finding places to have a good time, so distance was of no concern) for a night of hanging out with friends, drinking, dancing, and making some new friends. While I enjoyed going out to night spots, I never envisioned finding "Mrs. Right" in one of those night spots. No one in those places seemed to have the intent of creating long-term relationships that would evolve into marriage. Most of the men seemed to be in chaos over the numerous options of women, and most of the women seemed to be focused on what material advance could be made by connecting with a certain guy. My impression of many of those places was that they were more or less locations where everyone was looking to hook up. It was "all good," so to speak, when you're living it; but, in retrospect, life could have been enhanced in so many ways.

Here is where you find Russell and Cheryl, each one on their own path and living their best lives. Cheryl had been on a relationship rollercoaster having experienced the highs of marriage and then divorce. However, she had gradually regained her footing and wanted to wade back into the dating life. She was absolutely gorgeous and had no lack of suitors seeking her time and attention. She had sparingly given a few of those suitors opportunities to prove their seriousness and declare their longer-term intentions; however, none had advanced to the level of being her significant other. Cheryl had purposely focused her energy on her profession, and she was considering options for advancing her education by preparing to take the Law School Admission Test (LSAT). She was a lady who was about her business. So, if there was a Mr. Right for her, he needed to have his running shoes on because she was on the move.

It was the early part of summer on a warm June night. The club was jumping, and the music could be heard well before you entered the venue. As my roommate and I walked in, I paused and surveyed the entire club. It was a nice crowd; however, nothing stood out in my mind and I certainly didn't see any ladies that gave me a reason to take a second look. There were a lot of friendly faces with welcoming smiles, so I soon found myself engaged in a few different conversations. As the evening moved on, I noticed the crowd shift, expand, and the faces gradually change. On occasion, I would check in with my roommate and he would do the same. We always wanted to keep a gauge on the vibe to see if we should try some other night spots we were familiar with. However, it seemed we had decided to weather it out right there which was an indication that the conversations were decent and everyone was content. In one of my momentary pauses to survey the club, I noticed this incredibly stunning young lady standing between a young woman and man. My internal dialogue was, "WOW! She must be with dude."

Why was this beautiful creature in the club? I presumed the guy that stood beside her, her man, just wanted to show her off. But, with each of my discreet check ins, I noticed he never really engaged with her like they were together and she didn't engage with him either. When he took leave of her (for what I'll never know), I saw that as my opportunity to introduce myself. I had determined I needed to meet Ms. Gorgeous.

At a minimum, I had to know her name and how we might get to know one another if that wasn't her beaux. It seemed like the music got louder and the distance from me to her got longer than I initially calculated; however, my moves were intentional and deliberate. As I moved through the crowd and got closer to her, I could see that she anticipated my approach but wasn't going to give it away by looking directly at me. When I got to her, she was ready. I introduced myself and she in turn shared her name. I told her my plan. "I came over here to meet you and to see if we could be in contact." She reached into her handbag and handed me her business card. We were 23 or 24 years old and this lady pulled out her business card. I was impressed because at our stage in life, most people did not have business cards. I had never met someone in my age group who did. I was also impressed because it was the early 90's in North Carolina.

Since she was hanging out with her friends, I let her know I would be in touch and I bid her farewell.

It would be almost a month later, after a few telephone conversations and a couple of failed attempts to meet up, before we would actually see one another. Cheryl was very focused on her work and the potential of going back to school. I was focused on establishing myself as a military leader and a trusted resource as a strategic advisor for the unit. The meeting wasn't even a formal date but a gathering at the same night spot where the two of us first laid eyes on one another. I was serious about getting to know her because she was unique and reflected many of the qualities that I respected and thought would be difficult to find outside of the armed forces. Well into our marriage, Cheryl would acquire the nickname "The Lil General." We spent the bulk of that evening in conversation. The discussion was so intense that it seemed like the music had been totally silenced and the crowd had been dismissed from the club. We were very intrigued with each other. Over the next couple of months, we would spend a lot of time getting to know one another. While our time together during this period was unique and distinct to us, I don't believe it was anything that wouldn't be expected from two young people seeking quality human relations. It would be the time that followed those two months that would make our relationship special.

Later that summer, the world would be surprised to see Saddam Hussein and his Republican Guard invade the nation of Kuwait. Those actions would call to arms the United States military to protect its allies on the region and change the trajectory of our plans to move our relationship forward. The advent of the Persian Gulf War would see me preparing to deploy with my unit and Cheryl making the trek from Durham to share the last few days with me before I departed to fight in "The Mother of all Wars." I shared with my roommate that what I learned about Cheryl made me see her as the future Mrs. Williamson. Cheryl had no idea I felt this way. In kind, Cheryl felt I was Mr. Right. This was when the real development of our friendship began and created a foundational building block for the strength of our marriage.

The ten plus months that we spent apart during the Gulf War gave us ample opportunity to learn about our likes, dislikes, interest, passions, and goals. This was a period well before email, cell phones, texting, and social media. Our medium was pen and paper, and the slow exchange of snail mail across the sea and sand that separated them. What more powerful way to get to know someone and to share aspects of yourself than to have to put your authentic self on paper? Having to express everything you have thought about and felt since the last time you saw that person, or the last time you received a letter or a phone call (if while in the desert you happened to travel into some random, desolate location that happened to have a phone allowing international calls). There was certainly more than enough time for us to put all of their thoughts and feelings together and get them on paper.

In retrospect, each one of those letters was a part of the forthcoming agreement or contract that would be intrinsic to our marriage. The ideas, possibilities, and desires of our hearts were captured in those letters. They helped us know one another like few others would ever know us, including our parents. An early bond would be created that was invaluable and would be needed for the life we only envisioned and had yet to confirm. When I returned from the Gulf War, I was celebrated by my unit, my family, and Cheryl. I was oh so thankful for God's saving grace to have returned home in one piece. All the months of separation and waiting to see her again had come to an end and our reunion was everything they expected. The friends were together and could now think about and plan our future.

*"There are 'friends' who destroy each other, but a real friend sticks closer than a brother."*

*—Proverbs 18:24 (NLT)*

The friendship between us was established over the early years of our relationship and strengthened year after year throughout our marriage. It's common knowledge that developing strength usually only comes by providing a degree of resistance, like in weight training. It is the routine use of barbells and dumbbells to exercise one's muscles that develops strength over time. Our friendship and relationship have been tested over the years. The twists and turns of managing a growing family and establishing professional careers has brought considerable stress to who we are as individuals. Many times, its created questions in our minds as to the relevance of our marriage. We often wondered if it was worth enduring the challenges and sometimes even the successes to keep moving forward as a couple.

Our marriage took a turn for the worse after one corporate move. What we thought was a typical move, since moving had been frequent throughout our marriage, turned out to be the dismantling of everything we had worked for. We failed to communicate with each other our growing fears and resentment of moving again. Cheryl, the once ambitious career woman I met several years ago who had given me her business card, put her dreams on hold. We stopped being each other's best friend, and that led to us seeking validation from other people outside of our marriage. Our marriage has overcome infidelity. We survived betrayal, envy, and jealousy. We have lived through it.

When we failed to communicate with each other (for instance, Cheryl had issues with moving for the umpteenth time, yet she never shared those feelings), we set ourselves up to potentially be impacted by external forces such as relationships from the past and friends. We made the bad choices of allowing the wrong people into our family's inner circle. Those negative influences put our marriage at risk. We lacked transparency with each other and made poor decisions to share intimate details of our lives with others. Individuals who only had their own best interest at heart used those details to create chaos and confusion within our house with hopes of pointing us in the direction of divorce.

However, God had prepared us for such a time. We had to revisit the early years of our relationship and marriage and get back to the basics of what we had built our lives upon— our friendship. We had stopped sharing our likes, dislikes, interests, passions, and goals with each other. Instead, we had been sharing them with people outside of our marriage. When we first fell in love, it was because we chose faith in the other over fear of the other. Now we were faced with checking our desire to stay in love and that meant choosing humility over ego. We decided we wanted to remain true to our original desires of living life together, so we had to humble ourselves before God and before one another. We sought professional support with both mainstream and Christian counselors.

Love and friendship are choices. We had been riddled with bad choices that resulted in us betraying one another. The word betrayal often elicits images of physical or emotional affairs; however, betrayal also encompasses deceit and the manipulation of details and facts. These challenges come up and sometimes don't get the rigor of discussion they deserve. Then, a couple never gets clarity on the when, why, and how of the situations. Without clarity, there is an erosion of trust, confidence, and authenticity. Trust is certainly a tough bridge to build, even tougher once some parts of that bridge have been damaged. We see the building and improvement of that bridge as a daily process. Some days are better than others, but each day requires work.

We chose to love despite the difficulties we have faced, and we recognize the importance of bringing God back to the center of our marriage. We cannot overstate the need to have the presence of the Lord among us as the most integral cord. In a similar way, the power of our friendship could not be overstated. We may have once taken who we are to one another for granted, but we now treasure our friendship and are determined not to let that happen ever again. Each day we surrender ourselves to God and focus on putting Him and each other first.

We encourage all couples to invest in marriage counseling. That's right, it's an investment that will pay dividends. We had pre-marital counseling yet waited until we hit sandy ground to engage a marriage counselor. You've decided you want to spend the rest of your life with someone. We'd presume you want to grow, develop, and evolve over the years, and that's something you should be in total agreement about doing. However, you don't know what you don't know. So, having someone with professional training that could help you develop a life plan is a great starting point . Just like you would select a financial planner to prepare and plan for retirement, you want to provide yourself and your significant other with the proper tools and resources to have a productive and positive marriage.

If you've lived long enough, you've experienced the ups and downs of relationships of all types—father and son, mother and daughter, sister and brother, and the list goes on and on. Relationships are tough, but a commitment to love and establishing a friendship can endure what may in some instances seem insurmountable. Once you decide to be friends, that's when the work of friendship begins.

# Seventy Times Seven by Prayer and Faith

## MICHELE AND RODNEY PEAKE

*"Jesus said to him, 'I do not say to you, up to seven times, but up to seventy times seven.'"*

—Matthew 18:22 (NKJV)

## His Story...

Seventy times seven. I'm probably very close to that number for the amount of times my wife has forgiven me! When I said I do, I didn't realize how much I really didn't! I didn't possess the skills to be a good provider, a confidant, a friend; I didn't have what it took to be a good husband. Notice the most important word "good." My issues were a big obstacle to achieving that goal.

I had a wonderful childhood with a loving mother who taught me to respect women. She protected me from harm and danger and taught me life lessons. However, she couldn't teach me how to be a man. She couldn't help me overcome the fact that my father walking out on us when I was a toddler caused serious issues that neither one of us could see. The core problem that it caused was abandonment issues! I said core because there are a whole host of other issues attached to that one core issue. The abandonment caused me to feel like I was never good enough. How is that possible when I had a loving mother you might ask?

## Where's Dad?

Imagine going to a friend's house where the snacks are plentiful, there is always cold apple juice in the fridge, and his father is always willing to play catch. Meanwhile, back at home, my mom has to work overnight (making me a latchkey kid). There is food on the table, but the snacks are nonexistent. Apple juice were foreign words.

A situation I'll never forget happened when I was in the Boy Scouts. Every year, the Scouts had a wooden car derby race. They gave you a block of wood, four nails, four wheels, and some sandpaper. Then, they told you to go make a car. Well, my idea was to round off the sharp edges, hammer the wheels on, and *voilà*, you have a car! But when my mom and I showed up for the race, the first thing I noticed was that she was the only Mom there. The second thing I noticed was how creative and elaborate the other cars were. I asked a fellow Scout, "How did you create such a nice car?" His response was, "My dad helped me!" It felt like such a punch to the gut! While my mother was encouraging by telling me she loved the car I made and painted with nail polish because we did not have paint, I realized that Dads were very helpful in these areas. And I couldn't help but wonder for the first time in my life, where was my father and why doesn't he even call me? Did he not like how I looked? Was I too short? Was I too skinny? From the pictures, he was a fair-skinned man, so was I too dark? Those were the early signs of feeling abandoned.

## Abandonment

What I didn't know was that abandonment would lead to conflict avoidance, lying, and manipulation. But, I will get to that. To my mother's credit, she never said a bad word to me about my father. She wanted me to form my own opinion. (Great woman!)

When it was time to date, I introduced myself to girls as someone I wished I was. I wish I could say it stopped there, but it continued into my marriage. I was excellent at pretending. Pretending I wasn't damaged, hurt, and scared to be left. What I didn't fully realize was that I had qualities that were attractive to the opposite sex. My wife, for instance, fell for a guy that wasn't afraid to stand alone. I didn't buckle to peer pressure even though it cost me friends. I wasn't cool with following the crowd.

I would lie to cover-up the fact that I was a procrastinator. My constant answer was, "I did it." Knowing full well it wasn't done. The problem that compounded matters was I had conflict avoidance issues as well; so, when confronted regarding my procrastination and the problem it caused, I would run from the responsibility or find somewhere else to put it. This remained a constant problem in our relationship. Sometimes I would lie and ask myself, "Why did you even lie about that?" The person I wanted to be wouldn't have lied.

## *What's done in the dark*

What I know now that I didn't know then is that whatever is done in the dark will come to light. I can remember like it was yesterday that things began to turn around when my wife reintroduced me to my Lord and Savior. The first step was choosing a church, but more work needed to be done. She slowly began to change her life, and I started to follow. But my faith was tested when my mom passed away.

## *Generational curses*

After my mom's death, I reverted to very fleshly behavior. I shut my wife out and made myself emotionally unavailable to the world. The lies, procrastination, and manipulation started again; however, there was a new problem that arose. While my family was asleep, I began drinking Single Malt Scotch at $50 a bottle. I don't know what made my wife wake-up one night; but, about two weeks into my new habit, she woke up and took one look at me and the bottle and poured the scotch down the drain. The next night, I had another bottle and she woke up again and poured the contents of that bottle out as well. That night, God stopped my path to alcoholism (because I was surely headed that way).

I wish I could tell you that he removed my other thorns that quickly, but He has chosen to remove those very slowly and methodically. From that moment on, my wife has been praying for me, and I've been praying for myself. Through prayer, the tables finally started to turn. The first thing prayer helped me realize was that I was good enough. I prayed for

God to allow me to see my good qualities and why He created me. I loved myself, but He helped me to see that others could love me as well. One of the ways He helped me to see that was by reconnecting me with my half-sister, Benita. We talked, and she found out my father had eight more children, ten in total. He was married five times. I prayed to God to meet my other siblings, but for years it never happened.

One day, through my quiet time and prayer, I was told to forgive and connect with my father, Elliott. My praying wife said it was placed in her spirit too that I needed to connect with him. Huh? No. What I didn't know was that I needed to connect with him to show that I had truly forgiven him. I finally surrendered and connected with my father, Elliott, and it felt like a thousand-pound weight was lifted off of my shoulders. It was revealed to me that my issues were not only a result of my father leaving, but they were also from generational curses passed down by him. I finally knew what to include in my prayers! I began to pray for those curses to be removed. While I still have issues, they are not as strong in my life and my relationships as they once were. Prayer works!

One of my avoidance issues kept me from talking to my wife before making any decisions. Recently, during my prayer and quiet time, God told me to test what He had revealed to me about resolving a financial struggle. Ordinarily, I would use one of our accounts to solve a financial issue without talking to my wife. But, that morning was different. I went into our bedroom and told my wife about the issue, how I thought we should resolve it, and she agreed. I said to myself, "Wait, what?" Yes, she agreed. I followed God, and my wife and I were in agreement.

I am still in constant prayer that God removes my thorns completely. Prayerfully, I will be able to tell you one day that they are all gone. Until then, God is able and His grace is sufficient!

## Her Story

### In the beginning

In the beginning, I loved being a wife! We were high school sweethearts, so we got together when it was all about our looks and, for me, how into me he really was. As a young wife, marriage was fun! We traveled extensively and bought our first home together as an investment property, so bills were not a factor. We did not have children right away, so we could come and go easily. We were both young and in love and neither of us really understood, as I reflect back, the true roles of a husband and a wife as God defines them. So, I was in charge when I should not have been, and he let me when he should not have.

Today, 25 years later, I can't say that I have always felt this way about marriage. However, the love of my role as a wife today was birthed, in part, due to a greater understanding of the purpose God intended when He created the first couple, Adam and Eve.

It took me many years to begin to understand the role of a wife. And truth be told, I am still learning. One thing I discovered was that it was not what I thought it was. It was not an extension of dating where you only experience the best parts of a person. I recall feeling like I was on a long honeymoon in the beginning. I was married to my high school sweetheart who adored me. What could possibly go wrong? I was young, driven, and eager to start life as an adult with him. He seemed to always say and do the right things when we were dating and even into the early years of our marriage.

## When the tide started to turn

It wasn't until life's conflicts started to kick in (like having children, sick parents, and growing household responsibilities) that our long honeymoon phase came to an end. It seemed as if tough times brought out pieces of us that up until that point had remained hidden.

One of the things I started to experience was my husband not telling me the truth. I remember one time having what I thought was bank fraud because the balance in our joint account was less than what it should have been. I even called the bank to let them know someone withdrew money from my account and it wasn't me! When I confronted him on whether or not he withdrew the missing money, he told me no. I believed him until I discovered that it was in fact him who had withdrawn the money. Needless to say, I was shocked and devastated. Why would he send me on a wild goose chase?

Initially, I took his lying very personally. So much so that I questioned what was wrong with me that my husband would even want to lie to me. Soon, distrust set in and it was very hard for me to believe him regarding the simplest things. This soon caused our marriage to spiral out of control. We became distant emotionally, spiritually, and even physically.

God's Word says in Mathew 12:25 that "A house divided against itself cannot stand." Our division caused a lack of communication. On top of that, my husband lost his mom and our challenges escalated even more. Soon isolation set in. I felt lost and did not know what to do. I wanted to fix us, but I could not. I prayed and prayed.

How do you stay when you want to leave? What do you do when being married is no longer fun and you don't feel happy anymore? What do you do when things get so hard that you think to yourself, "This must have been a mistake. There is no way this is right! I'm sorry God, I messed up and went and married the wrong person." These were the thoughts that plagued me and kept me up many nights! I have cried myself to sleep while wondering what I have done wrong. Back then, I even questioned God while thinking, "He surely must be punishing me by not changing my husband."

*God can change things around in an instant*

One day, I heard God clearly say to me, "I know he may not be doing everything right, but when you stand before me, he won't be there. It will just be Me and you. So, despite him not being the husband he should be to you, without question, you must be the wife I purposed you to be. You will not be able to use your husband not doing his part as an excuse for you to not do your part." God told me that day to let Him work on my husband, and in the meantime, I could use some work on myself. The funny thing is that as I'm writing this, I recall that moment being so big for me that I called my girlfriend to share what God had just said. She asked me, as if she was asking for herself too, "What do you do while you're waiting for God to work on your husband?" I realized there are a lot of wives out there in the same position as me. My response at the time was, "When we find out, we should write a book!" How ironic that today I'm writing a chapter in a book. Only God!

From that moment on, it was like God began to open up my understanding about life, marriage, and more importantly Himself. I could see myself starting to put more of my focus on the God of the universe and less focus on trying to change the hurt, wounded husband I couldn't see when we were dating. As I started to seek God and He started to show me myself, it was like He took me by the hand (like a parent would do for a child) and started to walk with me while telling me to just take one step at a time. He showed me that I needed to get more of His Word in me. He showed me that I had to start talking and listening to Him more than I was listening to friends and family. He started showing me that there were things He needed to work out of me that were in the way of Him being able to use me to be the wife my wounded and hurt husband needed. He started showing me my own wounds and hurts, then He told me to give them to Him!

Healing and trust began to take place in my heart and in my husband's heart, and a ministry was even born out of that process. Not just a ministry for myself, but my husband also started working in ministry!

As I began to understand what grace was and that in your darkest moments that's all you have, I discovered that God's Word was correct. Grace is truly sufficient! As my relationship with God intensified, so did my trust in Him. My ability to lean more on Him with the big H instead of him with the little h grew. I started to see that it was possible to forgive. It was possible to submit. It was possible to love someone who did not seem to be loveable.

## Today

It's been a journey and a process to get to where I am now as a wife. Today, I seek Him first before I seek my husband. Today, my weapon of choice is prayer over arguing, trying to win, getting my way, or proving a point. I use my words more wisely now by not using them against my husband; instead, I use them against my real enemy. God tells us in Proverbs 18:21 that "Life and death are in the power of the tongue." God showed me that I was not responsible for my husband's actions, but I was not helping him either. In fact, my own hurt caused me to do things like befriend a gentleman I knew had bad intentions. God told me I had to keep quiet and only speak what He said, when He said. He told me I had to end the toxic relationship with the gentleman and avail myself to my husband without any distractions. I promise you, as soon as I did that, God turned things around for my husband and I. Previously, I felt invisible in my own house. After I was obedient to God by not talking so much and ending that toxic relationship, I felt like my husband started to see me again. I felt like I was no longer invisible. I started to see God working on my husband from the inside out. I started to see the truth in him prevail.

## Conclusion

The early challenges and struggles in my marriage drove me closer to Christ, helped me focus on my true purpose, and set me in the center of God's will for my life! And the truly amazing thing is that today my husband is also in the center of God's will for his life.

As he is letting God work on the wounds from his past hurt and pain of not growing up with a father by reading the Word and praying daily, I am also learning more and more each day how to surrender it all to God!

God has bought us both a mighty long way, and we have to say that prayer has been the largest component of that change. Two young people from East Orange High School who got runner-up for Best Couple were on the brink of destruction not once, but several times! But, God in His infinite wisdom saw fit to keep us together! We are no longer just existing, but thriving together in life, in His kingdom, in our home, and in ministry. Today, I am a licensed minister of the gospel, and he is a deacon in the church. And God is truly not finished with us yet!

The best for us is still yet to come, and we meet it with great expectations!

# The Importance of Service in a Relationship

## MAGNOLIA AND BRIAN COOK

*"... serve one another humbly..."*

—Galatians 5:13 (NIV)

The importance of service in marriage is almost as important as water is to the ocean. The vastness of our oceans means that they affect people all around the world. Besides providing enjoyment to millions of people, oceans also provide us with the air we breathe, the food we eat, and even the water we drink. Without water, all the creatures would die, humanity would starve, and life itself would be empty and dry.

When you define service in a marriage, many people may think negatively. Service? Some may equate that word with slave or servant; but, we equate service with humbleness, love, sacrifice, forgiveness, and understanding.

Throughout our years together, we have learned how to serve each other, our family, and God. Service is not an easy trait to possess. It is something that is acquired through trial and error. I recall times when we just didn't get each other. We argued the majority of the time and it was because we were both still learning the virtue of service. Having a service mentality does not render you as weak or as the subordinate. Actually, having a service mentality makes you a stronger person. Learning to be humble enough to put another's feelings and needs before yours makes and molds you into a masterful servant to your spouse.

The Webster's Dictionary definition of service is: the action of helping or doing work for someone. This is a black and white definition that sounds pretty simple; yet, it can be so much more difficult to do than this definition provides insight for. Service in a marriage relationship tends to have a much deeper meaning than making dinner for your spouse or taking out the trash. You might be thinking to yourself "No way!" or laughing, but service takes much more than a surface or outward action.

The word service is something that needs to be deeply considered before looking for wedding venues and buying dresses and tuxedos. Being happily married requires that one possesses the aptitude to always think of your spouse first in every situation. Service is not something that you can pretend to have for a few years, then it disappears and reappears according to the situation presented. It must be something that is in your very nature.

We both had to learn to submit to and serve each other. I know, those are bad words in this day and age. And no, we are not living in the Stone Age when women wore an apron all day, prepared food, washed clothes, and scrubbed the floors on their knees. We serve *each other*. We will share examples that have taught us to look out for each other and not focus on self. We'd rather focus our energy on each other, submit ourselves, and make an honest effort to put a smile on each other's face.

One of the secrets that we would like to share is to be comfortable with your spouse being the one that is shining. When *one* of us shines, we both shine! A couple of years ago, an opportunity was presented to my spouse to go on tour as the vocal director for one of the largest tours ever to hit North America. Panic was my first response. I thought, "What about me? How would I go through the school year alone? What if I got sick? Who would help me with the transportation for school events?" I was in such a selfish mindset, I couldn't even celebrate this amazing opportunity for him. Going on tour as a vocal director would be the peak of his already amazing career. But, all I could focus on was how alone I would be and who would look out for me. None of the thoughts that came to my mind included my husband's accomplishment. All I could think about was me! My service attitude had left the building. I didn't want to be happy for him. I wanted him to see how upsetting this was for me. I began to play the guilt trip game. So, instead of us enjoying that amazing moment, it was made to be a bad thing that could cause our marriage to end. I know, I was pretty dramatic! At that moment I forgot about all that we had endured together and that this was my best friend! If service had been the focus, what do you think the response would have been? We both would have been able to enjoy the excitement of embarking upon a new challenge. He would have been able to enjoy that moment of celebration. When service is not in the center of the marriage, ego, selfishness, and pride take its place. Service is such a small word with such a heavy meaning.

Let's share a major part of our marriage: the life and death of our son. It was such a tough time for our family. He was born so sick that the state labeled him as special needs because doctors couldn't come up with a diagnosis. So, it was a roller coaster for our family. We were in and out of major specialty hospitals for weeks at a time. Our son endured so much, and our family did as well. Imagine weeks without being at home, but trying to function as a family. We still had other children to raise and there was still a marriage to keep together. Time would be missed at work, which meant shortage of income. I wish there was a way to paint a pretty picture of this, but then you wouldn't get the real meaning of our chapter on service. We found ourselves sleeping in hospital rooms on a weekly basis, eating hospital food, and not seeing a bed for months. On top of all that, staying at a hospital became *very* expensive. We had to pay for parking, food, and travel because (again) we still had other children as well. This is when the vows that were said in the beautiful white dress and handsome tuxedo were tested. When sickness hit our son and life seemed unpredictable, service to each other was what saved our marriage.

All the years of health scares, hospital stays, and sleepless nights started to take a toll on our family. Our son was having, on average, fifty to seventy-five seizures a day. The specialists were at a loss for finding a medication that would control his epilepsy. We were under immense pressure twenty-four hours a day, seven days a week. We prayed, cried, and almost begged for a break for our son. Exhausted every day, we had no idea if or when we would have time to be a married couple.

Months and years passed, but there was no break. Service had to become the focus of our relationship. So, we started finding different ways to love and serve each other. Of course, we had to be pretty creative to keep our relationship afloat. Sometimes he would sing me a song, or I would go to the store and find a card that said exactly how I felt. There were times when our son would fall asleep, and we would slip down to the cafeteria and drink a cup of hot chocolate together. Service is finding a way to make your partner happy or giving them all of you no matter what. If both parties focus on serving each other nothing can stop the relationship from flourishing.

As time passed, our son's health continued to decline. We prayed, had faith, and became drained. As the mother, I think that I took watching our son's health fail in a much different way than my husband. I kept smiling through it. We had other children to live for, and I had a false sense of hope that our son would live longer than we would.

One day as we were driving in the car, we had an amazing conversation about what would happen if our son, Josiah, passed away. I had to let reality set in for a moment. Then, my husband took me by the hand and said, "Honey, it's inevitable that our son will not live long." My first reaction was anger! How could he speak against my faith? I said, "No way!" I prayed and asked God to heal our son. My husband looked into my eyes (with a servant's spirit) and said it again, "Honey, you already know the truth." I began to weep buckets of tears. I had to accept that our son's life was going to end. We weren't sure when, but he was no longer thriving. And when he began to lose bodily functions, the journey really took a turn for the worse. When we say that any and everything that could go wrong *did* go wrong, we are not stretching the truth.

Watching my family struggle for years was tough. To me, being the head of the family didn't mean that I was "in charge." To me, it meant that I needed to be the help and support that would keep the morale and energy of my family stable. Sharing with my wife that our son would pass away and that we had to be prepared for it was one of the toughest things I ever had to do. Wiping her tears, allowing her to be frustrated, and just being there was important for me as the husband and father. A life-changing experience for me was seeing how vital being a silent partner was. You know, as men, sometimes we forget that we need to serve our family. I couldn't expect to always come home to a prepared meal and a wife that was on top of the world. I had to serve the needs of the whole family. And through my servanthood, I was empowered each day to be the man my family needed.

We were labeled a special needs family due to our son's condition. Although he had amazing moments, his laugh was heavenly, and his smile was like looking into an angel's face, he just never thrived. His body didn't handle Earth well. I always say that he was too good for Earth to contain! What an amazing grace given to me by God that allowed me to be his dad. I learned service when our son was unable to hold his head up, walk, or even talk. I never thought I would be trained to be a nurse. We stopped being parents and became his medical team. This is major service! Many institutions offered to relieve our family. Even family members offered to adopt our son because they knew the hardships that came along with having a special needs child. But, I remember standing in the hospital room of a very well-known doctor in Baltimore as he gave us the grim medical prognosis for our son. We had no idea that he would need twenty-four hours of care. We both looked at the doctor and said, "We will take care of him." The doctor and his staff stood there in shock! We said, "Train *us* to take care of his needs." They began to ask us, "Are you sure?" And we both nodded yes.

Service is an easy word to say, but it is hard to do. The staff at the hospital stated, "You don't know what you are signing up for." We said, "Our son didn't ask for this." Our family was in agreement that no matter the cost, sacrifice, tears, or pain we would all go through it together. We stayed by our son through each operation, pain, seizure, and anything else that came along. Now, that's service to us. Putting aside being comfortable and willingly sacrificing your life for another person! Service and sacrifice go hand in hand. You can't have one without the other. It's like trying to eat peanut butter without jelly.

The Webster's Dictionary gives this definition of sacrifice: a destruction or surrender of something for the sake of something else; something given up or lost.

You have to be willing to make the sacrifice in order to be of service to your spouse and family. Once you are married, it is no longer about what you want, but what *we* need. Having Josiah in our lives, even though it was for a very short time (12 years to be exact), changed our innermost beings. We learned what real service and sacrifice was all about. We gained a well of wisdom from a little boy who couldn't speak. We learned wisdom about service and pure love.

# You Were Created to Worship

## KIMBERLY AND KEITH SOLOMON

∞

*"God is spirit [the Source of life, yet invisible to mankind], and those who worship Him must worship in spirit and truth."*

—John 4:24 (AMP)

The meaning of the New Testament Greek word most often translated worship (proskuneo) is "to fall down before" or "bow down before." Worship is a conscious effort to merge your body, mind, and spirit. Since it's an internal, individual, or corporate activity, it is recommended that you as a couple engage in this action both together and individually. God has a plan in reference to how you should worship together in your marriage regardless of place or situation. Many people reading this chapter will think that we are simply talking about the physical act of worship that occurs in church or in a special place in your house, but we are here to share with you the revelation that changed our lives!

## Sex

Yes, sex when two people engage in holy matrimony is considered by the Lord of lords to be a form of worship. It should incorporate selfless acts that glorify God with what He created on the inside of both of you. The enemy hates when God's couples come together on one accord and produce what He originally intended for them to produce. Anything God creates multiplies. It multiplies love, productivity, and focus on Him the Creator. So, with that being said, consider bumping up your worship in the bedroom as a defense against many of the enemies' fiery darts. When the bedroom suffers, every other part of your marriage is going to suffer as well. To most people this is a taboo topic, but God created us to worship Him in all we do. And, yes, all means ALL!

**The main goal of every good husband should be to lead and love, especially in worship.**

### All In

We are both veterans and have over 34 years combined service together in the USMC and the USAF. So, we understand the importance of getting in line and being on one accord.

*"Wives, submit yourselves to your husbands, as is fitting in the Lord. Husbands, love your wives and do not be harsh with them."*

—Colossians 3:18-19

Being all in does not mean that the woman is weak or that she is less than her husband. It simply means that God has designed and created an order that we must follow in marriage in order to achieve what He has destined for our marriage. The word "helpmeet" is actually a two-part word. Part of the word means protector. You need your protector with you in the battle. When a battle is about to take place, the military protectors line up and march to their place of battle. Before you go into battle in your marriage, you must be prepared for the march. You must be prepared for the challenges ahead.

Now, let us help you with what happens as you march. As you march, the leader calls the movement and the change step to get you back in line. If you don't get it after a few times, the person leading the march tells you to stop and start over. That is the same thing with God in your marriage. There have been times when God has said to stop and start over, but instead of starting over most people just stop and get a divorce. That is not the answer. Just because it didn't go your way doesn't mean you should get offended and quit. It means that you need to get back to a place of worship. Could it be that you weren't prepared for what God had for you at that moment? You are simply facing warfare that you were not equipped to handle. You are not alone; all marriages suffer from some sort of warfare.

## Warfare Worship

After six years of marriage, we are different fighters now. We used to have "heated fellowship" over the things that the enemy told us we couldn't change. We would fight about the communication and fight about the children, when in reality we needed to be fighting the devil. We needed to fight against what he wanted for our marriage. The enemy wished that our marriage wouldn't last and that we would give up on it. He couldn't destroy our marriage and he can't destroy yours, but he does want you to give it up. But, real fighters don't give up. They keep going until the last bell.

Look at any famous boxing match and think about how they train. Go back to the late nights before the match. Go to the locker room with the pep talks. Think about the long hours spent on practicing routines. Diet and exercise are key in any battle just as prayer and fasting is important in spiritual warfare.

As we began to research boxing, this is what we learned. Training to become a boxer takes effort, discipline, and self-confidence. When you are seriously considering boxing as a career, you need to join a gym and find a trainer. However, beginners can train themselves when they cannot afford a trainer. In general, a serious boxer should expect to train for three to five hours, three to five times a week.

## It Takes Effort

Now, let's apply that to your marriage. Training to become a boxer takes effort, discipline, and self-confidence. Can we tell you that those same principles will help you in marriage as well? Making a marriage work takes effort. It's going to take effort from both people involved. No person wants to carry the other person's weight all the time. No person wants to always pick out and cook dinner. No person wants to always be the better communicator. We understand that you weren't raised in a two-parent home, or you were raised in a two-parent home, but you still didn't get the right examples being taught in front of you. Let us help you out. The success of your marriage will take you putting some effort into your behavior and actions.

## It Takes Discipline

This is a sore subject for many people. Is discipline learned or are you born with it? We are military members, so we are familiar with discipline. To maintain our physical fitness standards and to maintain our sanity, it takes discipline. But, we didn't start out disciplined. It took a lot of work. The same goes for your marriage. In order to maintain success, you must be disciplined in praise, prayer, and worship. Are you willing to discipline your financial habits? Are you willing to discipline yourself? Here we go.

Self-discipline is a bad word for many of us because we think that it means cutting out all of our fun and erasing who we are. Even erasing who we pretend to be. But, that is simply not the case. When you are self-disciplined, you are actually making it better for your spouse. Your spouse can trust that you mean what you say. If you say that you're going to work and coming home, you are disciplined enough not to stop at the racetrack and spend the rent money! Which rolls right over into self-control.

Can you control yourself? Not just sexually, but physically and mentally. Can you incorporate a fitness routine into your daily living? Can you keep your mind focused on things above and not beneath?

*"Set your minds on things above, not on earthly things."*

—Colossians 3:2 (NIV)

Let's not confuse self-discipline or self-control with self-confidence. Self-confidence is a feeling of trust in one's abilities, qualities, and judgment.

## Self-Confidence

Why is it that many of us don't have self-confidence or on the other hand have too much confidence? We believe that many people don't know or don't understand the definition of the word. It's so important that we know definitions of words and how to use them. Words are powerful! It's the Word of God that should build our confidence not the world's idea of confidence. The world's idea of confidence is based on what you have that's temporal. God's idea of confidence is what you have that's eternal. Let's stop focusing on what's temporal.

Our marriages are worth more than simply the temporal things that we've acquired or will require. That's why so many people are focused on other people to build their confidence when in reality only God can build your confidence. A good friend of ours says, "People will build you up just to tear you down." You have to be careful not to let people build you up with their words just to turn around and tear you down with their words. When people have that much control over you, they will play you like a symphony in an orchestra. When God has control over your life, it is a beautiful composition.

## Symphony

At its best, marital worship is a unique combination of love and obedience. It's a skill which develops over time. As spouses worship together, they develop increasing sensitivity and cohesiveness. With the help of God, our visionary conductor, a disparate group of highly skilled individuals is forged into a team.

Whether you've been married for a number of years or are newlyweds, here are a few worship tips to consider:

1. **Know how your part fits.** Preparation goes beyond learning your spouse's needs and wants. Be sure to listen to your spouse. Understand how your part fits into the whole. Pay attention to seasons in your life where things change.

2. **Feel the rhythm.** Practice communicating with your spouse and pay attention to their needs and the larger focus other than what they are saying. When worshipping in your marriage, you need to feel a sense of collective rhythm. Be careful not to rush, especially in difficult transitions. Even when things in your life are going fast, you often have more time than you think. Anchor your marriage foundation on important facts. Organize and group your thoughts in ways which allow them to flow naturally. Don't forget to breathe.

3. **Pay attention to balance.** All marriages need balance.

4. **Play for the team.** Always be mindful that you're part of a collective sound. Never try to stick out.

Listen to your spouse and blend in with a oneness that only comes from you working together.

5. **"Music Police" kill the music.** If your spouse fails you during worship, don't point it out to your spouse. They probably also felt it and will try their best not to repeat it. "Worship Police" can create a debilitating and backstabbing atmosphere, which kills real music making. Never react to a failure, especially in the act of worship. Just stay in the zone of worship.

6. **Where you sit isn't important.** Every part of your marriage is essential. Don't compare your marriage to those marriages around you. Be careful not to covet other relationships as well.

7. **Enjoy the sound around you. Your marriage was formed by God to make a beautiful sound of worship unto Him. Enjoy it!**

Often times in our relationships we can get caught up in what's not working and forget what we were created for. In our family dynamic, we have eight children, two baby mothers, and two baby fathers. Most people don't understand how we have managed to make it work as a family; a blended family. We have learned the revelation that our worship determines our altitude. Our worship opens doors. Our worship brings answers. Our worship is more than just an act that we engage in to satisfy ourselves; it is a holy time of worship unto the Lord. Yes, it takes sacrifice. It takes waiting patiently on God.

God is saying to us, "Wait on me. Be my server. Serve me. Don't sit still. Refill my drink. Check on my people.

Check on what I want done in the earth. Deliver my people. Take notes. Take my order. Give me your best. I want the best seat in the house." We are here as servant leaders on this earth to serve our Lord. We serve Him best when we have a healthy worship routine with our spouse.

## 10 Tips to Help You Foster Healthy Worship with Your Spouse:

### 1. Beware of non-verbal communication

Your posture shows if you are present or not so present. Your posture should reveal if you are willing or not so willing. Non-verbal communication is very important!

Maintain eye contact to ensure that you engage to the best of your ability. The eyes are always telling a story.

Don't make yourself the victim. Never claim that you are the victim. The Bible tell us that we are more than conquers; so, let's get out there and engage the heavenliness, giving the living God legal right to move on our behalves.

### 2. Over communicate when sharing new ideas

In reference to worship with your spouse, this will help foster an environment ripe for true worship. God desires couples to worship Him in Spirit and in truth. There is a thin line between maintaining your personal worship life with God and maintaining a healthy worship life with your spouse. If done correctly, you can maximize your intimate experiences with God and with others, taking all that you do to the next level.

## 3. Avoid relying on visual aids instead of words to communicate that you're ready for worship time

- ▶ Use colorful, descriptive words to make your point
- ▶ Use non-verbal clues
- ▶ Don't always avoid the obvious
- ▶ Get straight to the point

## 4. Ask for honest feedback

Ask your spouse or kids how you are doing as a spouse and as a parent. Kids are more prone to tell you the raw truth. They don't mind being honest with you despite the chance of getting in trouble. Let them express themselves and be open.

Allow your spouse to be open. It's important to hear how your spouse feels about you. You may think you are doing well, but in reality you may be below the standard that God has set in His Word.

## 5. Engage your family in discussion

Pick a time (dinner time or a time that's convenient for everyone) each day to discuss family issues and accomplishments. Sit down with the family all together. Make a meal and have everyone talk about their day. Talk about the good, the bad, the ups, and the downs.

## 6. Express yourself

Make sure you repeatedly express yourselves to each other. Depending on each person's learning style, it may take more than one time for them to get it. Sometimes you have to express your ideas and rules to your family more than once. Maybe your spouse didn't grow up in the same structured environment that you are used to, so they are learning structure for the very first time. Think of your marriage in terms of age.

A one-year marriage is a newborn and can't do anything on its own. It needs a lot of help, support, and assistance.

A three-year marriage is a toddler. It's still exploring its new environment, but it's more independent. It's growing and beginning to realize its power.

A ten-year marriage thinks it's good. It's made it past the newborn, toddler, and kindergarten stages. It's elementary qualified. You may only have to repeat your points to it once because it gets it the first time around.

Regardless of the age of your marriage, don't get discouraged. If your spouse won't listen to you, take them to God spiritually. Tell God in prayer what's going on, and let Him work it out. You can't change other people. You can't expect other people to change because you are changing or expect them to communicate the same way that you do.

## 7. Master the art of timing

This is so important. You shouldn't wait until you are in the midst of "heated fellowship" to bring up all of the issues you have with your spouse. Don't wait until you're in "heated fellowship" to blow up about your sex life or their gambling problem. Take into account the timing before trying to conquer everything. No problem was birthed in one single swoop. They all followed a process—a thought, then a word, then an action.

## 8. Get to know your spouse

Your communication can be the most effective and better received when you understand who you are talking to and tailor your language to that person. Just like a tailor gets the measurements before making a garment, you must do the same. The tailor realizes that all people are not made the same; they vary in height, weight, etc. We have to think the same way and know that we can't communicate with our spouse like we communicate with our children. We can't even communicate with all of our children the same way. Each child is different. I'm even suggesting that communication varies from marriage to marriage. Each marriage is different. Even if you were in a good relationship and now you're in a new good relationship, there's a good chance that the communication style has changed. Those two people may not speak or think the same. You have to be careful not to compare them or make the new spouse pay for the last spouse's downfalls in communication.

## 9. Focus on respect

In relationships, all people want to be respected. Everyone wants their chance to be correct. Everyone wants the opportunity to know that they are doing the right thing and that they can be trusted as a leader. It takes confidence in yourself to respect your spouse's gifts and talents. Confidence to know that their strengths don't diminish you or make you smaller. Confidence to know that they are not trying to make you feel dumb. Confidence to know that their method of communication may be flawed and it's not about you. You may begin to label yourself as a bad communicator because of other people's flaws. But, rather than point out their flaws, focus on respecting them at their level. God will eventually show them the plank in their eye, but it is your job to love them. Men equate love with respect and women equate love with protection.

## 10. Be a listener

Listen more than you talk. God gave us two ears and one mouth for that very reason. The problem is that many of us want to talk all of the time and be heard! It's okay for you to be quiet and let your spouse talk. We must first listen to what others have to say before we can make an informed comment or decision. It's not informed if you don't have the information. How many times have you said something that you know once released had nothing to do with the speaker's original statement? This can cause you to develop resentment and ill feelings toward one another, pushing you further away from unity in worship.

Now that you understand the importance of being all in, warfare worship, and communicating with your spouse, it's time to come up with a strategy for your worship. The strategy is to go into the spiritual realm. Demons are assigned to keep you from getting revelation. They are assigned to people and regions. But, in the spiritual realm, you will get the revelation you need to grow.

We want to leave you with this important piece of information: when God desires to birth something in the spirit realm, He requires intimacy; physical intimacy for man and wife. In Genesis, God hovered over the face of the deep. The Hebrew word used for hover is rachaph. This same word is used to denote the manner in which a husband hovers over his wife before sex.

Just as worship is crucial in the bedroom, praise is crucial for both husband and wife to feel desirable in each other's eyes. Adoration for one another creates the atmosphere. Praise happens in the outer court. You often hear praise and worship because if the spouse isn't praised before you get into the bedroom, it will be hard to get worship out of them in the inner court. Everyone isn't welcome in the inner court. Instead, it's the intimate place for you and your spouse to become one, to leave a lasting impact in the spiritual realm, and to shake Heaven and hell. Come on! The angels are rejoicing! You were created to worship!

# Sources

*Merriam-Webster's collegiate dictionary.*
Retrieved from http://www.merriam-webster.com

Scriptures marked AMP are taken from the Amplified Version®. Copyright © 2015 by The Lockman Foundation. All rights reserved.

Unless otherwise indicated, scripture quotations are from the Holy Bible, King James Version. All rights reserved.

Scriptures marked NIV are taken from the New International Version®. Copyright © 1973, 1978, 1984, 2011 by Biblica, Inc.™. All rights reserved.

Scriptures marked NKJV are taken from the New King James Version®. Copyright © 1982 by Thomas Nelson. All rights reserved.

Scriptures marked NLT are taken from the New Living Translation®. Copyright © 1996, 2004, 2007, 2013 by Tyndale House Foundation. All rights reserved.

Scriptures marked CSB are taken from The Christian Standard Bible. Copyright © 2017 by Holman Bible Publishers. Used by permission. Christian Standard Bible®, and CSB® are federally registered trademarks of Holman Bible Publishers, all rights reserved.

# About the Authors

**Shirley Walker-King and Vincent D. King**

Vincent and Shirley met in San Diego, California. Vincent was stationed on board the USS Tuscaloosa while serving in the United States Navy, and Shirley worked for the California Department of Corrections. Vincent, now retired from the United States Navy, works for the United States Postal Service and holds a bachelor of science degree in business administration from Northwood University. Shirley is the CEO of SWK Management and Consulting Services, a talk show host, and a producer. Shirley holds a bachelor of science degree in human relations and business from Amberton University. She is also certified in mediation and dispute resolution, and human resources and organizational development.

The King's, married for 27 years, are certified facilitators in several relationship curriculums and love sharing relationship skills, tools, and techniques that will inspire couples to like, love, and lead each other with great intentions. Vincent and Shirley have one daughter, Valencia King.

Learn more at www.ShirleyWalkerKing.com

## Raquel and Turhan Jones

Turhan and Raquel M. Jones have been married for fourteen years and have four boys together. They own and operate Internet Radio Stations, DFWiRadio and DFWiGospel.com. Both companies are thriving and changing the Internet Radio Market. They are opening DFWiLatino.com in 2019. Turhan, an extraordinary music producer, has been a musical genius since birth. He has produced over 300 songs for various music artists. He is a studio engineer, records music, composes songs, and mixes them. He manages a recording studio and the daily operations for DFWiRadio and DFWiGospel.com. Raquel hosts her own show on DFWiRadio.com, "The Newdayze Show," handles the accounts for both stations, social media, marketing, and administration of the companies. Raquel is a poet, writer, and has a book, *Let Thy Vibes Be Good*, coming in 2019.

To connect, email them at info@dfwiradio.com

**Kaldejia and Robert Faulk**

Dr. Robert Faulk and Lady Dee Faulk are the founders and pastors of Faith Tabernacle World Outreach Center in Sumter and Bishopville, South Carolina. Faith Tabernacle, one church in two locations, was founded in 1997. Their mission as pastors is to increase God's family with people transformed by His Word, showing compassion to Christ's body and outreach to the world as they glorify God through worship. In addition to their pastoral duties, their goals are to foster unity among the races, fellowship among churches, and rebuild the wastelands in Sumter, Bishopville, and surrounding counties.

Dr. Faulk and Lady Faulk are bestselling authors in the anthology *Souled Out* and are members of Destiny Life Ministries International (DLMI) and the Association of Independent Ministries (AIM).

Learn more at www.faithtabernaclesc.org

## Tyria D. and Kenneith E. Jones

Tyria D. and Kenneith E. Jones currently reside in Houston, Texas, with their youngest daughter, Kiara. They have been happily married for six years. They have seven amazing children and five adorable grandbabies. Kenneith and Tyria have felt the call to write as part of their ministry to help men and women overcome obstacles and live victorious lives. In 2015, Kenneith encouraged Tyria to share her story and write her first book, *A Crown of Beauty for Ashes*. She is currently working on her second book project as well as other collaborations. Tyria also encouraged Kenneith to do the same and he is currently writing his first book. Together they started *Tyria D. Jones LLC* in 2018 and desire to one day launch a nonprofit organization that will help women escape domestic violence situations. They currently lead a small group for married couples to help them have more fulfilled relationships.

Learn more at www.tyriadjones.com

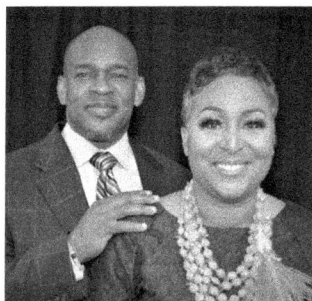

## Cheryl and Russell Williamson

Cheryl and Russell Williamson have been married for twenty-six years. Together they started Williamson Media Group and their nonprofit organization, Soul Reborn. Cheryl and Russell were featured at the 108[th.] NAACP National Convention and Congressional Black Caucus, they are the producers of The Power of Laughter Heals the Soul comedy series, and they produced their first stage play in 2018. As authors of multiple bestsellers such as: *Soul Reborn, Soul Talk Volume 1 and 2,* and *Soul Bearer,* Cheryl and Russell have won two Indie Author Legacy Awards for 2017 Literary Trailblazer and 2018 Anthology of the Year.

Cheryl earned her degree at Shaw University while Russell has degrees from West Point, Troy University, The Wharton School of the University of Pennsylvania, and Southern Methodist University.

Cheryl and Russell have three children and two grandchildren. They are passionate about pouring into others, their faith, and leaving a legacy.

To connect, email them at cheryl@cherylpwilliamson.com

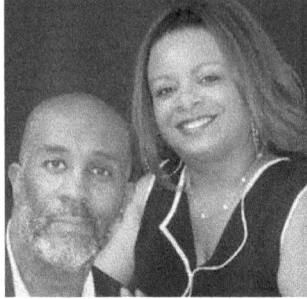

**Michele and Rodney Peake**

Michele and Rodney are high school sweethearts who have been married for over 25 years. They have two daughters, Zarina and Nia. They have both won several public speaking awards with Toastmasters International. Rodney is a deacon and Michele is a licensed minister at Mt. Calvary Baptist Church where they serve on several ministries together. In addition, Michele is a certified life coach and author with over 20 years of leadership experience with Fortune 500 companies and several nonprofit organizations.

Rodney is a successful playwright and director who has written a full-length screenplay and written and performed eight stage plays. He has enjoyed being a technician with a Fortune 50 company for 20 years. In 2018, Rodney and Michele started Peake Point Productions. In March of 2018, Rodney suffered a major stroke, but by the grace of God he is on the way to a full recovery.

To connect, email her at mnoelpeake@gmail.com
and email him at thedirectorofmore@gmail.com

**Magnolia and Brian Cook**

Brian and Magnolia Cook are a true power couple that loves God, family, and one another. They work together in the gospel music industry and own "The Studio Spot" recording studio where prices are made affordable for those who may not have the larger budget to record their project.

Brian and Magnolia have overcome disappointments, death, and divorce. They have learned the true meaning of love and friendship by experiencing failures and successes. They are so pleased to be a part of this project.

Learn more at www.thestudiospot.net

**Kimberly and Keith Solomon**

Keith and Kimberly Solomon are ministers ordained by God and driven by a passion to help others "Be their best!" They are fully certified neurolinguistic practitioners and relationship and life coaches, helping clients achieve their personal and professional goals. The essence of their work is to facilitate self-improvement and growth by helping people identify their core challenges and self-limiting thoughts. Keith and Kimberly founded the outstanding ministries My Brother's Keeper and My Sister's Keeper united as one ministry through Keepers International. Their vision for Keepers International encompasses marriage, family, and relationships. Their mission is to empower and facilitate deliverance in others so that they can live their best lives. Their passion is to take God's Word to a hurting and lost generation.

Learn more at www.keepersinternational.org